CONTENTS

Preface ● 4

Introduction ● 5

Project Preparation ● 6

Appliqué Techniques ● 8

Projects ● 13

A Coloring Spell ● 15

My Own Place Mat ● 35

Touch Me, Feel Me, Read Me ● 41

Counting on Buttons ● 57

Rolled-Up Fun ● 65

Finishing Basics ● 69

Gallery of Quilts ● 73

About the Author ● 79

PREFACE

In 2001 I had the great opportunity to publish a book with Martingale & Company based on a quilting technique that is dear to my heart. This simple method for creating machine-appliquéd pictorial quilts is called *repliqué*, a word I came up with by combining *accurate replicas* with *machine appliqué*. My book *Repliqué Quilts: Appliqué Designs from Favorite Photos* was a smashing success and a delightful learning experience for me. That book has since gone out of print, but I have continued to use the repliqué technique in many different ways. However, none of my new projects were quite right for a second book until a very special event took place in January 2006. On the 21st of that month, God blessed me with the ultimate inspiration: I became a grandma when Hanna Lucille Colwell was born in Pasco, Washington. This event gave our family great joy tempered with a bit of frustration, because her grandpa and I live in Watertown, Wisconsin. With Hanna so far away, I filled the "I miss Hanna" moments by designing and making quilts for her.

Hanna's first quilt was made before she was born—a simple design of squares and hearts made up in flannel. After meeting her when she was five days old, I felt I needed to make a special quilt just about her. "Hanna's Bedtime Quilt" was the result (see page 73). Inspired by a quilt made by my friend Roberta Williams, I tried my hand at poetry (having grandchildren will make you do unusual things!) and decided I wanted to ink the words directly onto the blocks. The creatures in the poems all have meaning for Hanna and her family. I created a small "Hanna" doll, and each block needed a pocket for the doll to crawl into. No grown woman should be allowed to have this much fun, and repliqué made the process easy. "Hanna's Bedtime Quilt" was a joy to create and a joy to present to Hanna when we went to visit her when she was five months old.

Upon returning from that trip, ideas for quilts with words made just for kids kept flooding my head. After making "A Coloring Spell" (shown on page 14) for Hanna, it hit me that other adults might want to make educational quilts for kids too, and the idea for a second repliqué book was born.

I hope you have as much fun making these projects as I had designing them. It's also my hope that you will imagine your own versions of Snuggle-and-Learn quilts. Some of my friends and students did just that, and their work is displayed in the "Gallery of Quilts" beginning on page 73. May God bless you and all the special children in your life!

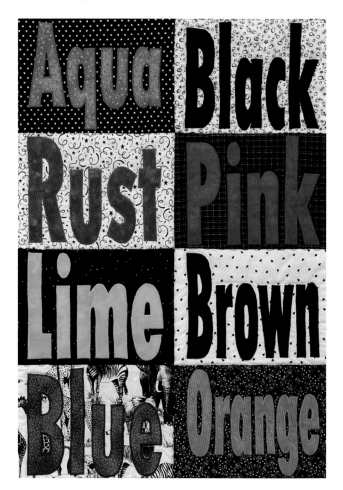

INTRODUCTION

If you're looking for patterns for kids' educational quilts, you're in the right place. Here you'll find quite a variety of projects. Most likely the hardest part will be deciding which one to make first, so we'll begin with some basics while you make up your mind.

The first chapter will get you started. It guides you through choosing fabric, thread, and supplies, but probably the most important portion of this chapter is about patterns. Be sure to read over the different pattern-making methods before beginning any project, especially if you plan to personalize it.

The second chapter presents two different methods for appliqué; I encourage you to choose the technique you prefer. This chapter includes lots of information concerning machine appliqué. If you are new to this process, you will appreciate the details that give your stitching a professional look.

Now it's time to make the decision: which project will be your first? If you're not sure, "My Own Place Mat" on page 35 might be a good place to start, because it's small and uses basic techniques. "A Coloring Spell" on page 15 would be a good choice too, but it's a bit bigger. After appliquéing all those colors, you'll be quite proficient! All the other projects are fun to make, and each has a few unique and exciting twists. Hopefully you'll pick up some tips along the way that you can use in all your quiltmaking.

Don't pass up the gallery on page 73. You will find not only the quilt that started it all, which I made for my granddaughter, but a few other projects I've done with the repliqué technique. Then comes some real fun—seeing what imaginative things other quilters have done with the ideas presented in this book. Hopefully it will get you thinking about venturing off in your own direction.

Since this is, after all, a quilt book, it is essential to include tips and techniques for finishing the quilt. Whether your project will hang on the wall, sit on a table, or cover a child, there is information here you won't want to miss. Please don't forget to make a label for your quilt. It's the last step and—in my estimation—essential.

PROJECT **PREPARATION**

As any quilter or sewer knows, there is a certain amount of preparation that must be done before the stitching can begin. For these quilts, creating and and/ or printing the patterns is an important first step. This may be a bit more time consuming than just picking a quilt pattern off the shelf at your local shop, but completing a unique project for a special person is worth the extra effort.

This chapter also covers gathering supplies and selecting fabric and thread. While you may be familiar with these tasks, be sure to read these sections, because they offer information specific to the repliqué technique.

CREATING PATTERNS

Some of the patterns used in this book are printed at full size and simply need to be photocopied or traced. Whenever a project is personalized, or when you prefer a different font, you'll need to create a pattern. Have no fear—there are options! If you are adept at drawing your own letters, grab a piece of paper and have at it. If you are not comfortable drawing freehand, check your local library where you will likely find books with alphabets in various fonts and styles to trace and enlarge. Your computer is another source for alphabets, numerals, and other patterns. Instructions for creating patterns with your computer follow.

Remember to Reverse!

Whether you're creating patterns for traditional fusible-web appliqué or for repliqué, it is important that the pattern *always* be a mirror image of the finished quilt. This is especially critical when using numbers and letters. If you're creating your own patterns for words, be sure to reverse them either by placing them wrong side up on a light box before tracing or by scanning them into a computer and making a mirror image of them before printing.

Creating Letter and Number Patterns Using the Computer

I have found that the Microsoft Word program creates great patterns. If you don't have this program, perhaps you can adapt these instructions to your computer or find a friend with Word.

A Word about Fonts

There are many different fonts available in Word. Narrow or intricate fonts can be difficult to appliqué. For best results, use a bold, chunky, sans serif font for your letters.

1. Open Word. A blank page will appear in a portrait (vertical) orientation. This works well for a single number or letter. Click on File at the upper-left corner of your screen to change the orientation to landscape (horizontal) for a whole word or collection of letters or numbers—and to adjust the margins (which you will want to do!). Click on Page Setup, followed by Landscape. While there, also change all margins to 0.5". Click OK.

2. If the drawing toolbar isn't visible on your screen, click on Tools on the top taskbar. Click on Customize, and then select Drawing. The drawing toolbar should now be visible at the bottom of the screen.

3. To create the pattern, click on the Insert WordArt icon (the icon has a slanted letter *A*) on the drawing tool bar. Select the box with outlined letters in the upper-left corner of the WordArt Gallery window and click OK. The Edit WordArt Text window will appear. Type in the letter, word, or number you wish to make into a pattern. The default font will appear in the Font box at the top. Use your mouse to scroll through the list of fonts and select a clean and simple font for appliqué. When you've highlighted the font you want, click OK.

4. The typed word will now appear in the upper-left corner of the blank document. Click on the word and a box will surround it. To enlarge the word pattern, place the cursor over the lower-right corner of the box, hold down the left mouse button, and drag the box to a spot about ½" from the lower-right corner of the page. Continue to adjust the pattern in this manner until you are pleased with its size and placement.

5. To reverse the pattern, click on Draw on the drawing toolbar. Click on Rotate or Flip and then on Flip Horizontal. The pattern is now ready to print.

GATHERING SUPPLIES

Basic sewing supplies are all you need to machine appliqué. You probably have most of these items already on hand, but if not, check for them at your local sewing-machine dealer or fabric store.

- Basic sewing supplies (dressmaker's shears, straight pins, seam ripper, pencil, and so on)
- Sewing machine with the capability to do a zigzag stitch and an adjustable stitch width and length
- Darning or free-motion presser foot. You'll need to disengage or cover the feed dogs when using this foot so you can move the fabric in all directions.

Check your sewing-machine manual to see if you need a special throat plate.

Darning foot

- Appliqué or satin-stitch presser foot. This foot has a wide opening to accommodate a side-to-side zigzag stitch. The raised area on the bottom of the foot creates a tunnel for the stitches to pass through. An open-toe appliqué foot is especially helpful since there is no bar in front of the needle to obscure visibility.

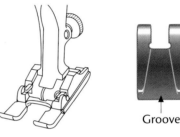

Groove

Appliqué foot

- Rotary cutter, mat, and rulers. My favorite rulers are a 6" x 24" rectangle and a 12½" square.
- Thread in a variety of colors to match fabric (see "Selecting Fabric and Thread" below)
- Transparent tape
- Embroidery scissors with a sharp point
- Paper-backed fusible web (required for traditional fusible-web appliqué; not required for the repliqué technique). There are a number of these products on the market. Look for one that can be stitched and has paper on one side only.

SELECTING FABRIC AND THREAD

When making kids' quilts, I primarily use 100%-cotton fabric that has been prewashed. The only time I use other fibers is when a specialty fabric is required to get the right effect. Unique textures are what make "Touch Me, Feel Me, Read Me" (shown on page 40) work—for example, I used polar fleece for *Fluffy*, flannel for *Soft*, netting for *Rough*, and so on. The chalkboard fabric is what makes "Kade's Rolled-Up Fun" (shown on page 64) so much fun!

Bright colors add childlike playfulness to these projects. Enjoy choosing just the right colors for "A Coloring Spell" and colorful, high-contrast fabric for "My Own Place Mat" (shown on page 34).

Bright colors enhance the impact of "A Coloring Spell" (shown on page 14)—and encourage learning too!

I find that cotton thread works best with cotton fabric. The best look for appliqué is achieved by matching the color of the thread to the color of whichever fabric is on top (the appliqué fabric, or the background fabric if you are doing reverse repliqué). The closer the color matches, the better the stitches will look.

Matching the bobbin thread to the top thread guarantees a good result, even if your tension isn't perfect. If you find it tiresome to fill that many bobbins, another alternative is to fill only three bobbins: one each with a light, medium, and dark thread. Match the value of the top thread to the bobbin; for example, use light thread in the bobbin when you are using yellow thread on top, and use dark thread in the bobbin when you are using navy blue thread on top.

APPLIQUÉ TECHNIQUES

Two different appliqué methods can be used for creating Snuggle-and-Learn quilts: traditional fusible-web appliqué or my repliqué technique. Please read the instructions for both techniques and decide which one best suits you and your project. Both yield great results, but I prefer to use repliqué in my Snuggle-and-Learn quilts because it doesn't require fusible web or any other fusible products. Fusible web tends to make a quilt stiffer; thus, a finished quilt made with repliqué is softer and "snugglier." Also, since the appliqué pattern and fabric can be layered on the background (or behind it, for reverse repliqué) in one piece, it eliminates the need to cut and fuse the multiple small pieces required for fusible-web appliqué.

This section includes detailed instructions for the necessary methods. Whichever technique you use, be sure your machine is free of lint and in good working order. If you are new to machine appliqué, it will be helpful to have the manual for your machine close at hand.

PAPER-BACKED FUSIBLE WEB

1. Select a paper-backed fusible web and place it paper side up on top of the pattern. Trace around the characters, figures, or shapes on the pattern. (These will be referred to simply as *characters* from now on.)

2. Cut out the tracing, leaving at least ¼" of excess fusible web all the way around.

3. Place the fusible web glue side down on the wrong side of the appliqué fabric and press, following the manufacturer's instructions.

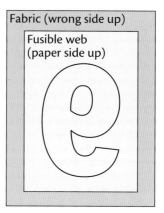

Fabric (wrong side up)

Fusible web (paper side up)

4. Cut out the fabric pieces directly on the traced lines. Remember to cut out the interior, open areas of any characters.

5. Remove the paper backing, position the appliqué fusible side down on the background fabric and press, following the manufacturer's instructions. This fuses the appliqué to the background fabric.

6. Secure a stabilizer of your choice to the back of the block and satin stitch around the appliqué. When the appliqué is complete, remove the stabilizer.

REPLIQUÉ

1. Center the pattern right side up on the wrong side of the background fabric and secure at the corners with pins or transparent tape.

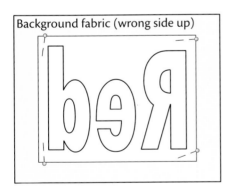

2. Turn the unit from step 1 over so the background fabric is face up, and place the appliqué fabric wrong side down on the right side of the background fabric. Secure with pins or tape. Hold this unit up to the light and view from the pattern side

to make sure the appliqué fabric covers all the characters on the pattern.

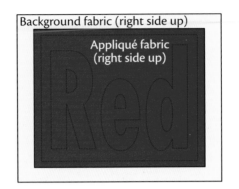

3. Turn the unit over and use a free-motion straight stitch as described on page 11 to stitch along the lines of each character on the pattern. Use thread on the top of the machine to match the *color* of the appliqué; use thread in the bobbin to match the *value* of the appliqué.

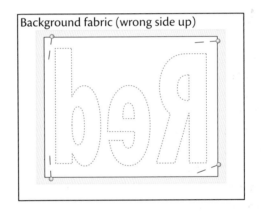

4. Turn the stitched unit to the fabric side and carefully trim away the appliqué fabric very close to the stitching. Remember to trim out any interior areas.

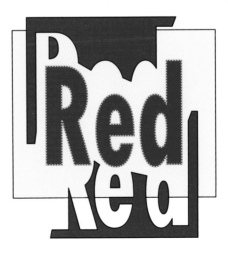

5. Satin stitch as described on page 11 around all the characters in thread that matches the color of the appliqué fabric, making sure to cover the raw edges of the appliqués with one side of the stitch and to cover the bobbin thread from the previous free-motion stitching with the other side of the stitch.

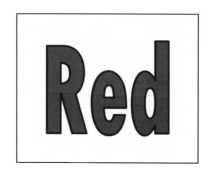

At some point you will need to remove the paper pattern. I do this at different times during the process, depending upon the project. The individual project instructions will guide you in doing this.

TRIMMING TIP

During the trimming step, the raw edges are a bit fragile prior to satin stitching and can pull away from the straight stitching if handled too much. Therefore, I prefer to trim a few areas at a time and then satin stitch those edges before continuing to trim another area.

REVERSE REPLIQUÉ

In repliqué and traditional fusible-web appliqué, the motif is stitched on top of the background. In reverse repliqué, the motif is created by cutting away the background fabric and allowing the appliqué fabric to show through. Reverse repliqué is especially helpful when you're using fragile or difficult fabric for the appliqué, such as the tricot lamé in "Touch Me, Feel Me, Read Me" (shown on page 40). The challenging fabric is captured and satin stitched *beneath* the background and thus stabilized.

1. Place the background fabric wrong side up on your work surface. Place the appliqué fabric right side down on the wrong side of the background fabric and secure with transparent tape. (The wrong side of the appliqué fabric will be facing up).

2. Center the pattern on the wrong side of the appliqué fabric and secure with pins or tape.

3. Use a free-motion straight stitch as described on page 11 and thread to match the background fabric to stitch along the lines of each character on the pattern.

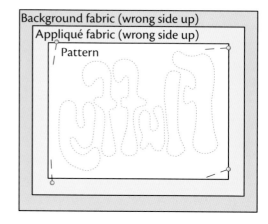

4. Turn the stitched unit to the fabric side and carefully trim away the background fabric from inside the characters. Trim very close to the stitching.

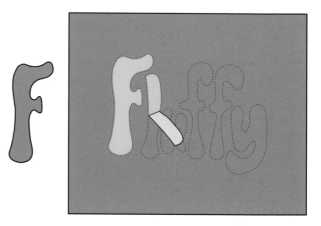

5. Using thread to match the color of the background fabric, satin stitch as described on page 11 around all the characters, making sure to cover the raw edges of the background fabric with one side of the stitch and the bobbin thread from the previous free-motion stitching with the other.

THE STRAIGHT STITCH

When you first turn on your sewing machine, it automatically defaults to the straight stitch. The feed dogs are engaged and typically the stitch length is set to 10–12 stitches per inch. You will use this stitch mainly for piecing blocks together, adding borders, and attaching bindings.

When used with a walking foot attachment, the straight stitch is a great way to machine quilt a project with straight-line quilting.

THE FREE-MOTION STRAIGHT STITCH

Free-motion stitching is most commonly used to quilt the layers of a quilt together. However, in repliqué, it is the stitch you will use to sew along the lines of any design that has lots of curves and corners. If you are new to free-motion stitching, this is a great way to give it a try, because these stitches merely baste the appliqué fabric in place and are eventually covered with satin stitching. Therefore, even if your free-motion stitches aren't perfectly even or exactly on the line, no one will ever know!

Just imagine the needle is a pencil, the fabric-and-pattern unit is the paper, and you're attempting to draw by moving the paper under the pencil.

1. Drop or cover the feed dogs according to your machine's manual.

2. Attach the darning or free-motion presser foot to the machine.

3. Place the fabric-and-pattern unit under the needle. Bring the bobbin thread up to the top anywhere along the pattern line by making one complete stitch and pulling on the top thread tail while also holding the top thread above the eye of the needle. The bobbin thread will pop through to the surface. Hold both thread tails as you begin to stitch.

4. Stitch along the line of the character on the pattern until you return to the spot where you began. Move to another character and repeat until all the lines have been stitched.

THE SATIN STITCH

This stitch can be used for both traditional machine appliqué and my repliqué technique. Refer to your sewing machine's manual to prepare the machine for zigzag stitching. Since children's quilts are usually used, washed, and loved a lot, it is important that their construction be sturdy. To accomplish this, a fairly wide satin stitch is a must! The wide stitch takes a big bite of the appliqué fabric, thus securing it well to the background. Somewhere between $^3/_{16}$" and $^1/_4$" is a good stitch width.

Adjust the stitch length so the stitches are close enough together to create a smooth, even satin stitch as shown. When the stitch length is set at 0, the feed dogs do not move the fabric at all. The satin-stitch setting on most machines is a range just before 0. A very short length makes the stitches very close together and gives a fine, finished look. The short length does, however, create many needle holes close together, which may weaken the fabric. The stitches should be close enough together to look attractive, but not right on top of each other.

| Straight stitch | Zigzag stitch | Satin stitch |

Do not adjust the top tension until you have made some test samples. If puckering occurs, loosen the top tension in small increments until the stitches lie flat.

Check to be sure the feed dogs are engaged (they may be lowered from the previous straight stitching) and thread the machine to match whichever fabric is on top (the appliqué fabric for traditional fusible-web appliqué or repliqué, the background fabric for reverse repliqué).

Practice Makes Perfect

If you have never free-motion stitched before, make up a sample and practice, practice, practice! Try to establish a rhythm between your hands, which are moving the fabric, and your foot, which determines the sewing speed. You will most likely feel awkward at first (most quilters do), but keep at it, because improvement comes quickly.

Stabilizing

With the repliqué technique, the paper pattern acts as a stabilizer and no additional stabilizer is necessary. However, when using the satin stitch to finish the edges of traditional fusible-web machine appliqué, pin or tape a piece of scrap paper or use a purchased tearaway, wash-away, or heat-away stabilizer of your choice beneath the block.

Begin stitching on any right-angle corner or—if the pattern shape doesn't have a corner—along a straight line on the pattern. Make sure the satin stitch completely encases the raw edge of the appliqué.

Stitching Corners

Corners can prove tricky if you've never appliquéd before. Practice stitching with scraps on stabilized fabric before proceeding to your project.

Outside Corners. Satin stitch to the corner of the shape and stop with the needle down on the *appliqué side* of the stitching at the point shown in the diagram below. Lift the presser foot and turn the piece to stitch the new edge. With the presser foot still raised, manually turn the hand wheel to raise the needle. Continue turning the hand wheel until the needle swings to the opposite needle position; then slightly shift the piece and lower the needle back into the hole it just emerged from. Lower the presser foot and continue stitching. The stitching lines will butt together at a right angle, avoiding the bulk of overlapped thread at the corner.

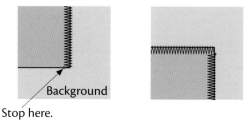

Stop here.

Outside corner

Inside Corners. Satin stitch past the corner the distance of one stitch width. Stop with the needle down at the point shown in the first diagram at upper right. Lift the presser foot and turn the piece to stitch the new edge. With the presser foot still raised, manually turn the hand wheel to raise the needle. Continue turning the hand wheel until the needle swings to the opposite needle position; then slightly shift the piece and lower the needle back into the hole it just emerged from.

Lower the presser foot and continue stitching. The stitching lines will butt together at a right angle, avoiding the bulk of overlapped thread at the corner.

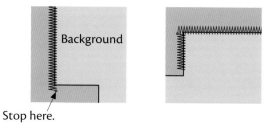

Background

Stop here.

Inside corner

Stitching Points

Points are simply sharp corners, and they look best when there isn't any bulk at the tip. To achieve this, satin stitch down the first side of the shape until the needle is swinging into the background on both sides of the point, as indicated by the asterisk in the first illustration below. With the needle down, raise the presser foot and pivot the piece slightly so the point is aiming toward you. Lower the presser foot and continue stitching, gradually decreasing the stitch width to 0 as you reach the point. Lift the presser foot and turn the piece to stitch down the second side. Set the machine for a short, straight stitch, and stitch in the background, close to the edge of the appliqué, until you reach the spot marked with an asterisk. Raise the needle and set the stitch width to the original satin-stitch setting. Resume stitching, being aware of the right and left needle positions.

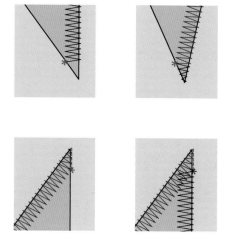

Satin-stitched points

PROJECTS

It was so much fun creating the quilts for this book!
I began by thinking like a grandma to come up with
educational themes that would be enjoyable for me to
appliqué and also good learning tools for kids. Colors,
numbers, animals—the list went on and on. Narrowing
it down to just five designs was the toughest part! Once
I had chosen my favorites, I switched to thinking like a
child to choose the colors, fabric, and little extras that
would give each design its unique "kid appeal." As the
process continued, I became aware that the concept
and techniques would lend themselves to projects that
weren't just snuggly *quilts*, thus the patterns for a place
mat and play mat. Each brought a whole new dimen-
sion to my idea of quilts for kids.

Even if you don't plan on making all the projects in the
book, I still encourage you to read through each one.
You may find something—an idea, an inspiring tip—that
will come in handy at some point in your quiltmaking.

A Coloring Spell by Chris Lynn Kirsch

A **COLORING** SPELL

This bright quilt is a wonderful way to teach a child about colors. The checkerboard of black-and-white background blocks provides an exciting field for the colorful words. You can use a variety of black-and-white background prints, as in the sample, or create a slightly less busy look by choosing just one black and one white print. Fabric amounts are given for both options. Whichever option you choose, be sure the black fabric contains just a bit of white print and the white contains just a bit of black, for texture. In this quilt, you want those colorful words to star!

Finished Quilt: 39" x 46" ● Finished Block: 11" x 8"

MATERIALS

Yardage is based on 42"-wide fabric. Fat quarters measure approximately 18" x 21".

½ yard of black solid for folded inset border and binding

⅓ yard *each* of 15 different-colored solids or tone-on-tone prints for color-name appliqués and strip-pieced outer border

8 fat quarters of assorted black-with-white prints for block backgrounds*

7 fat quarters of assorted white-with-black prints for block backgrounds*

2½ yards of fabric for backing with horizontal seam **or** 2⅞ yards of fabric for backing with vertical seam

43" x 50" piece of batting

2½ yards of 18"-wide paper-backed fusible web (not required for repliqué technique)

*If you prefer, choose just two background fabrics, one black-with-white print and one white-with-black print. You'll need ⅞ yard of each.

Which Colors?

For the quilt on page 14, I used pink, aqua, lilac, black, yellow, red, rust, blue, orange, green, white, brown, peach, purple, and lime. You may substitute other colors of your choosing, but avoid color names with more than six letters (such as turquoise), because it's difficult to fit them in the blocks.

CUTTING

Cut all pieces and strips across the fabric width.

From *each* black-with-white print, cut:

1 rectangle, 9" x 12" (8 total)*

From *each* white-with-black print, cut:

1 rectangle, 9" x 12" (7 total)*

From *each* different-colored solid or tone-on-tone print, cut:

1 rectangle, 8" x 12" (15 total)**

2 strips, 2" x 25" (30 total)

From the black solid, cut:

2 strips, 1" x 42"

5 binding strips, 2½" x 42"

If you are using just one black and one white print, cut 8 black rectangles, 9" x 12", and 7 white rectangles, 9" x 12".

**Cut these rectangles for the repliqué method only. For paper-backed fusible appliqué, you will cut the letters individually.*

MAKING THE BLOCKS

Some colors look best against a black background, while others look best against white. Pair up each 8" x 12" different-colored rectangle with the 9" x 12" background rectangle of choice before beginning. Refer to "Appliqué Techniques" on page 8 for guidance as needed.

1. Photocopy or trace the full-sized color-name patterns on pages 19–33 to create pattern sheets for repliqué, or trace the letters onto fusible web for paper-backed fusible appliqué.

2. Use either the paper-backed fusible appliqué method or the repliqué method to create each color name on its 9" x 12" background rectangle. If you're using the repliqué method, remove the paper pattern from the wrong side of each block. If you are using the paper-backed fusible appliqué method, remove any stabilizer.

3. Press each block well from the wrong side using spray starch and steam.

4. Trim each block to 8½" x 11½", making sure each color name remains centered in its background rectangle.

PUTTING IT TOGETHER

1. Arrange the blocks in five horizontal rows of three blocks each, alternating the black and white rectangles as shown below.

2. Sew the blocks into horizontal rows; press. Sew the rows together to complete the quilt center.

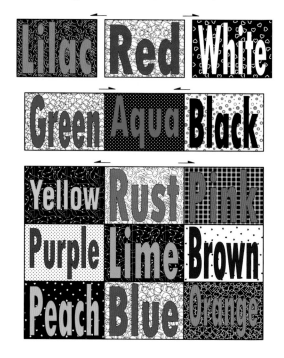

MAKING AND ADDING THE BORDERS

1. Sew the 1"-wide black strips together end to end; press. From this strip, cut one strip, 1" x 33½", for the bottom folded inset border and one strip, 1" x 40½", for the right folded inset border.

2. Press each inset border strip in half lengthwise, wrong sides together.

3. With right sides together and raw edges aligned, pin the 33½"-long folded strip to the bottom edge of the quilt top and machine baste in place with a ⅛" seam allowance. Repeat to machine baste the 40½"-long folded strip to the right edge of the quilt top.

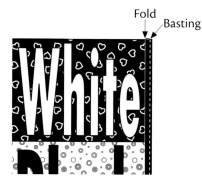

Fold
Basting

4. Arrange one of each color of the 2"-wide colored strips side by side. Select the 10 most brightly colored strips; set the remaining five aside for another project. Remove the same five colors from the second set of 2"-wide colored strips.

5. Arrange one set of the 2"-wide colored strips you selected in step 4 in a pleasing visual arrangement. (The border on the quilt shown on page 14 loosely follows the colors of the spectrum.) Sew the strips together along their long edges to make a strip set; press. Make a second, identical strip set using the second set of colored strips. Crosscut the strip sets into a total of seven segments, each 6" wide.

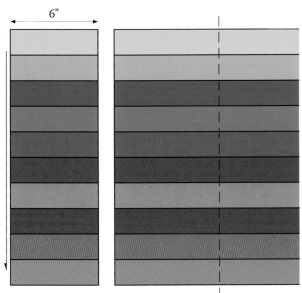

Make 2 strip sets.
Cut 7 segments.

6. Sew three segments from step 5 together to make a bottom border strip. Press the seam allowances in one direction. Sew four segments together to make a right-edge border strip; press.

7. Place the right-edge border strip right side up beside the right edge of the quilt, aligning the short end of the border strip with the upper-right corner of the quilt. Place the bottom border strip right side up beside the bottom edge of the quilt, aligning the short end of the border strip with the lower-left corner of the quilt. Shift the border strips as needed so the colors at the lower-right corner match up when folded at a 45° angle to make a

miter. Trim the border strips at the top and/or left edge as necessary to allow for this adjustment.

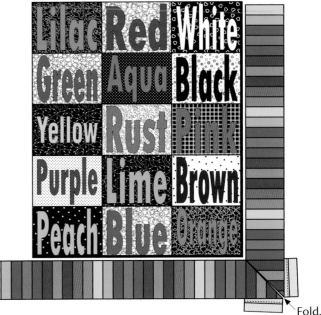

Fold.

8. On the wrong side of the quilt, mark a dot ¼" in from the lower-right corner of the quilt center. With right sides together, stitch the right and bottom borders to their respective sides, beginning at the nonmitered edge and stopping with a back-stitch ¹⁄₁₆" before the marked dot. Press the seam allowances toward the quilt center.

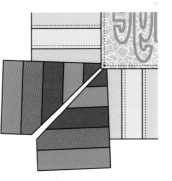

No More Puckers!

To avoid having a pucker where the three seams (the quilt center and the two adjacent borders) meet, it is important not to sew beyond the marked dot when adding the borders and not to sew into the seam allowance when sewing the diagonal, mitering seam (page 18). If you stop and start ¹⁄₁₆" before the dot or from the end of the border seam, puckering should not be a problem.

9. Fold the quilt top in half diagonally, right sides together, aligning the border strips on top of one another as shown. Place the long edge of a 24"-long acrylic ruler along the diagonal fold, aligning the 45° line on the ruler with the long border seam.

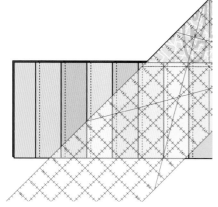

10. Use your preferred marking tool to draw a line along the edge of the ruler, from the end of the border seam to the outside edge of the border strip. Pin along the marked line, making sure to line up the seams in the pieced borders. Stitch on the marked line, beginning 1/16" from the end of the border seam.

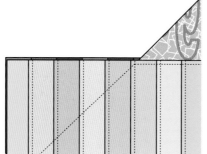

11. Check the miter from the right side to be sure it lies flat. Trim the seam allowance on the miter to 1/4", press to one side, and then press the border seam allowances away from the quilt center.

FINISHING

For detailed instructions on finishing techniques, refer to "Finishing Basics" on page 69.

1. Piece the backing, and then layer the backing, batting, and quilt top. Baste the layers together.

2. Hand or machine quilt as desired. I machine quilted over the seams between the blocks with a walking foot and a pre-programmed machine serpentine stitch. I then free-motion quilted around each color name by dropping the feed dogs and using a darning or free-motion quilting foot.

3. Square up the quilt sandwich, trimming the batting and backing even with the quilt top.

4. Use the 2½"-wide black strips to make and attach a binding to the quilt.

5. Add a label to your quilt.

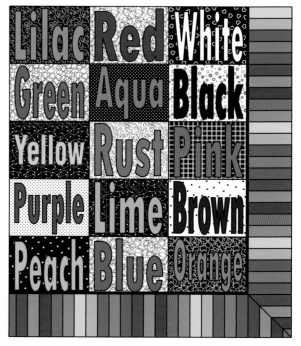

Quilt plan

A Generous Idea

I know of many quilters who enjoy making quilts to help others. This pattern makes a great choice for charity quilts for children, and if you choose to omit the folded inset and pieced rainbow borders, it's even quicker and easier to make. I know of one guild that made these borderless quilts as a workshop activity.

This is a simple project to prepare in kit form, because only a small amount of fabric is needed for each color name. Organizers can purchase one yard of each color-name fabric and precut each into 12 rectangles, 8" x 12", which is enough for 12 kits, each containing one of each color-name fabric. The background fabric can also be purchased and precut and added to the kits, or participants can provide their own black-and-white fabric.

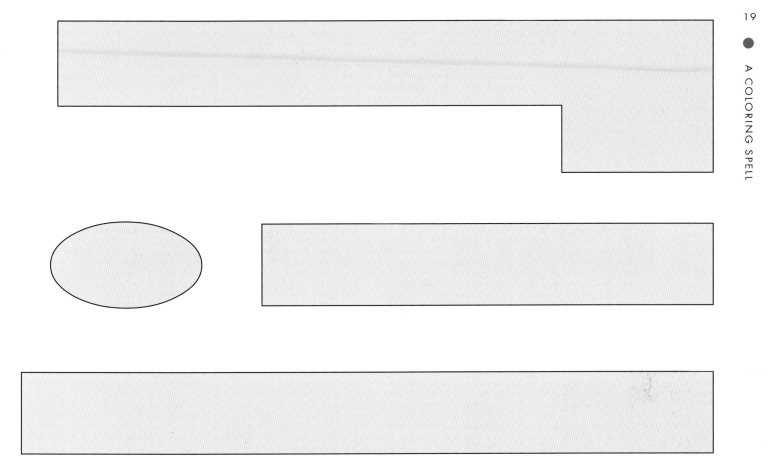

• PATTERNS ARE FULL SIZED •

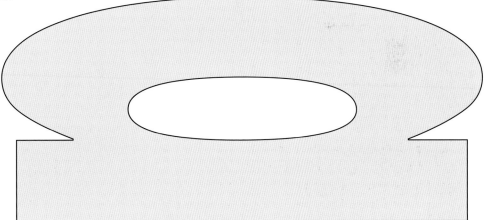

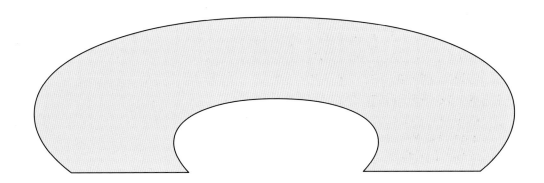

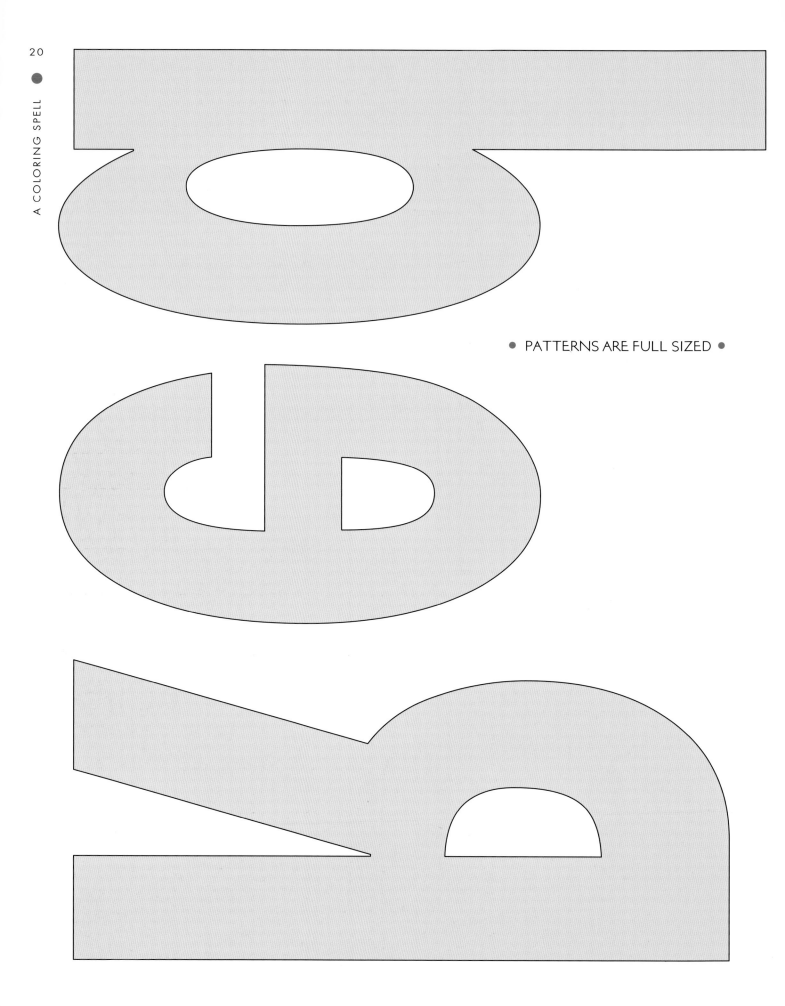

● PATTERNS ARE FULL SIZED ●

● PATTERNS ARE FULL SIZED ●

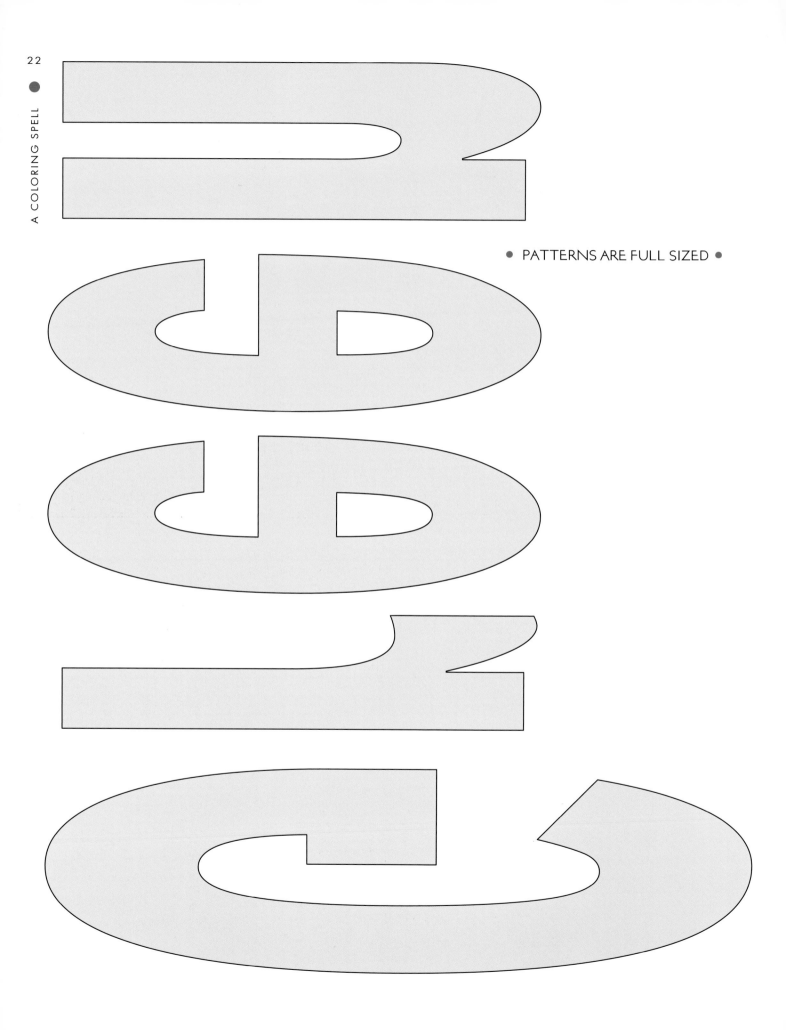

● PATTERNS ARE FULL SIZED ●

• PATTERNS ARE FULL SIZED •

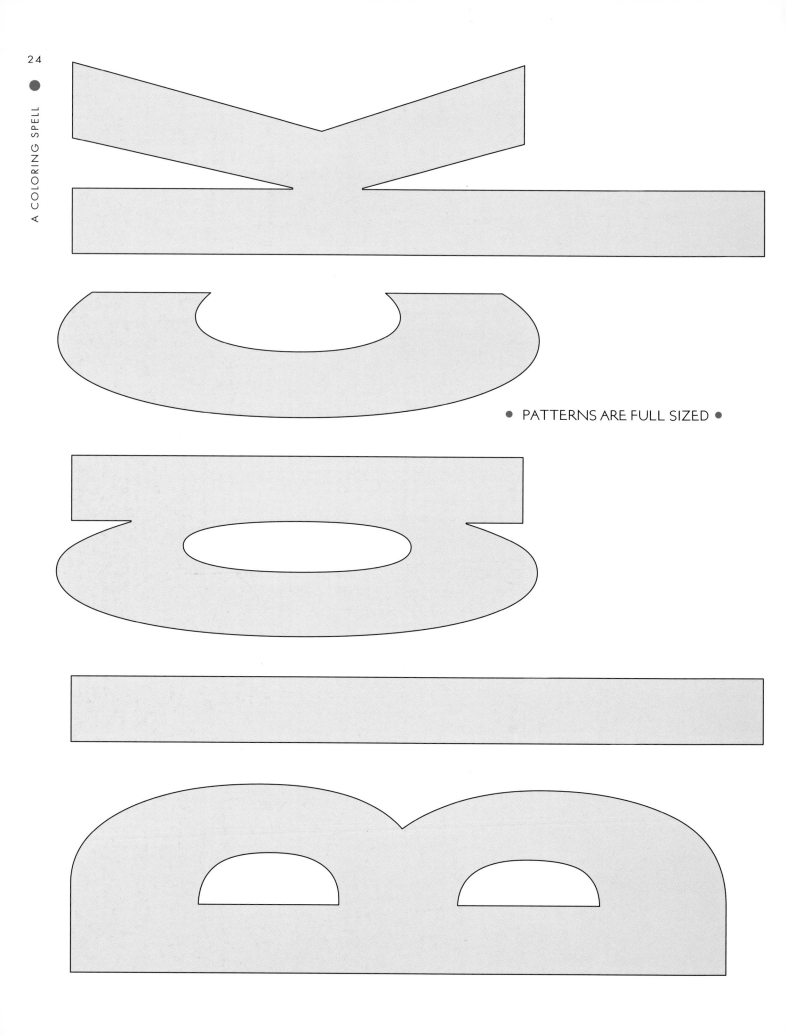

● PATTERNS ARE FULL SIZED ●

● PATTERNS ARE FULL SIZED ●

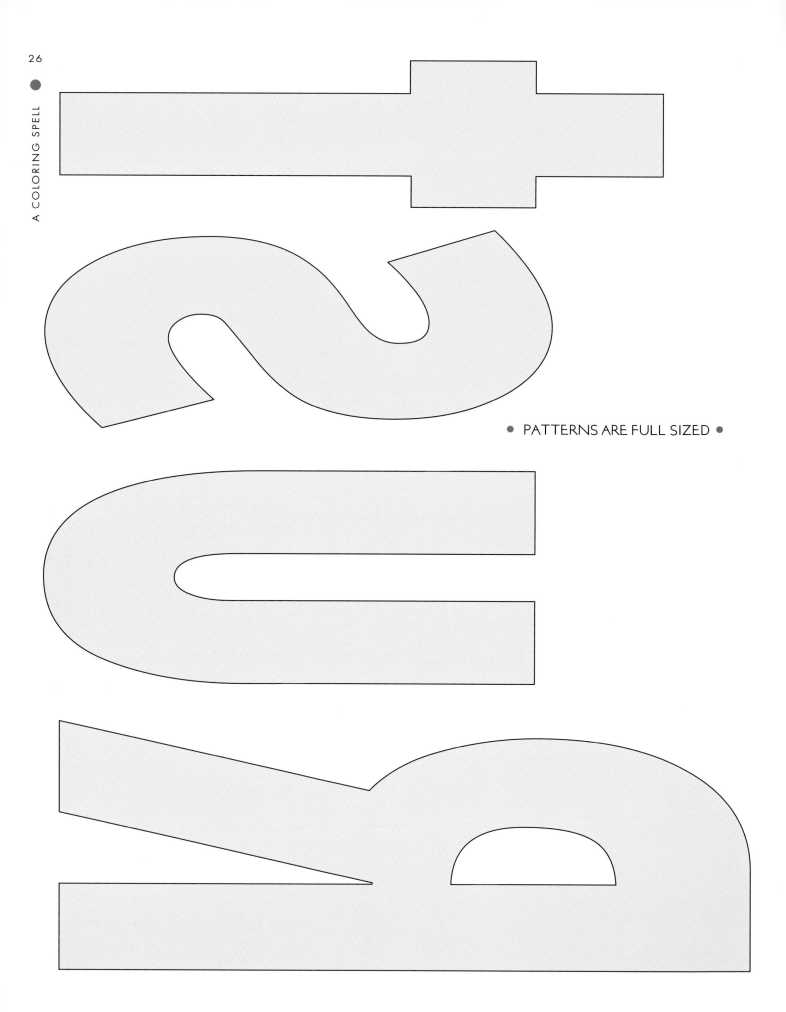

● PATTERNS ARE FULL SIZED ●

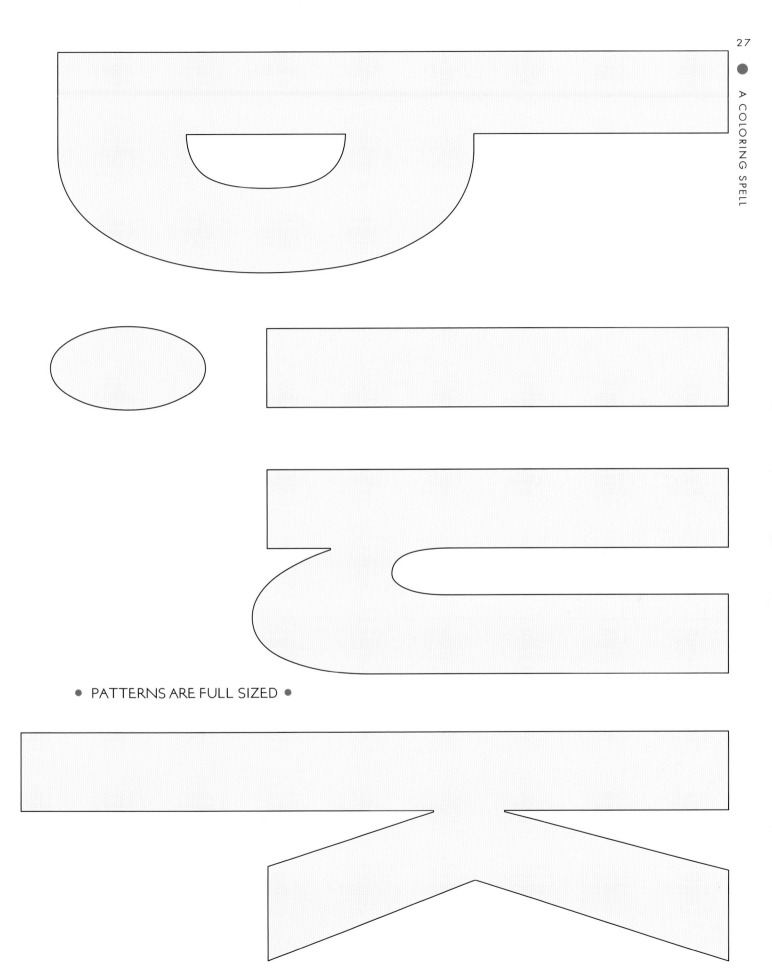

● PATTERNS ARE FULL SIZED ●

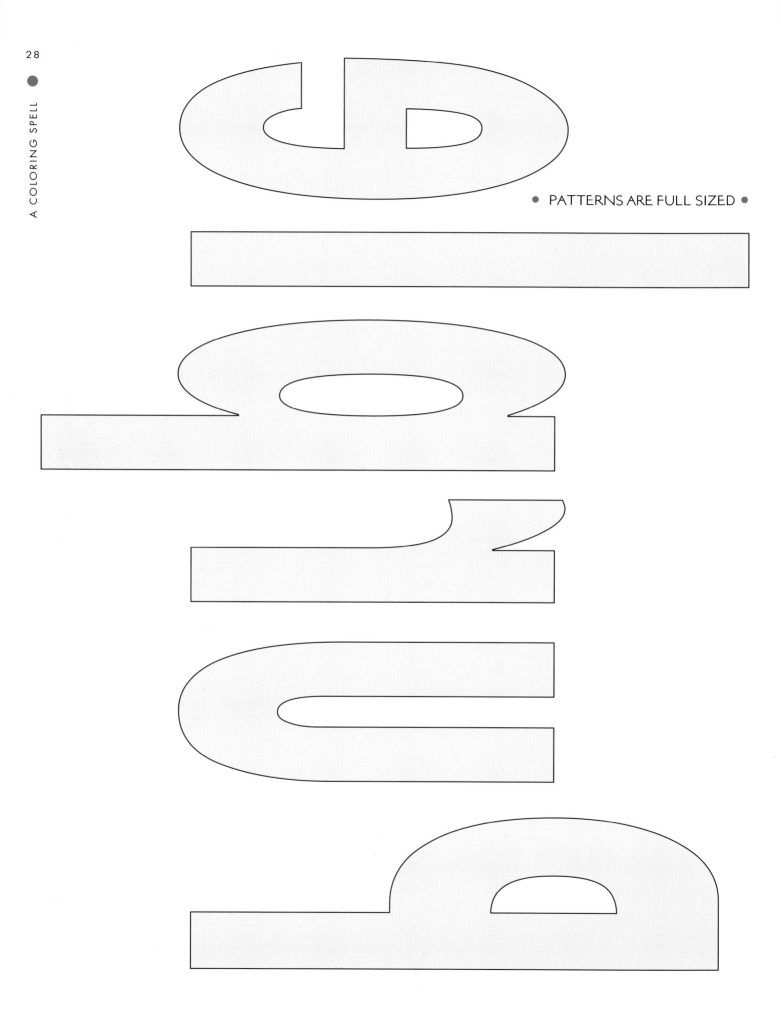

● PATTERNS ARE FULL SIZED ●

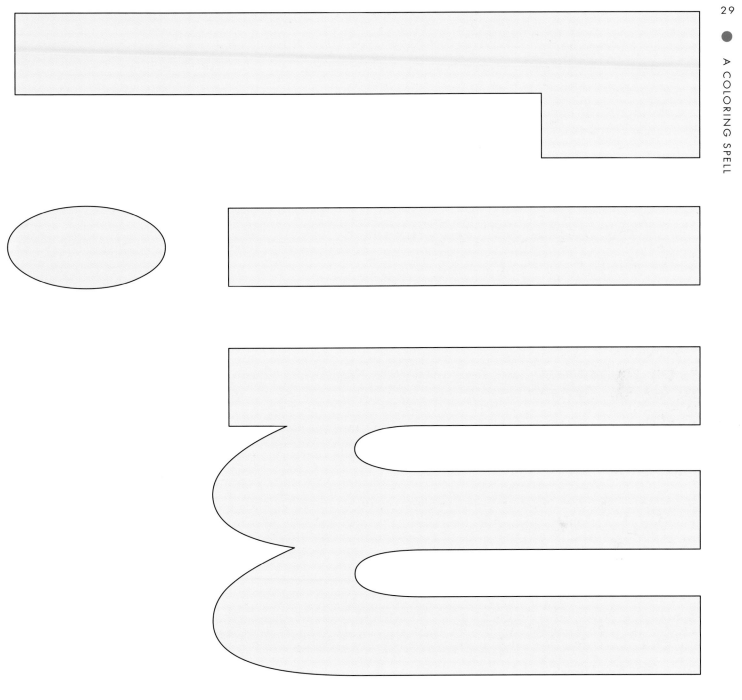

● PATTERNS ARE FULL SIZED ●

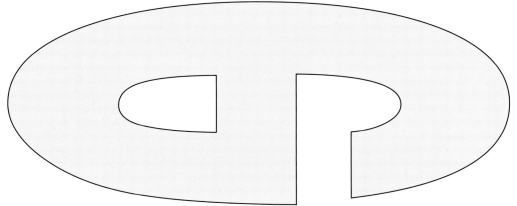

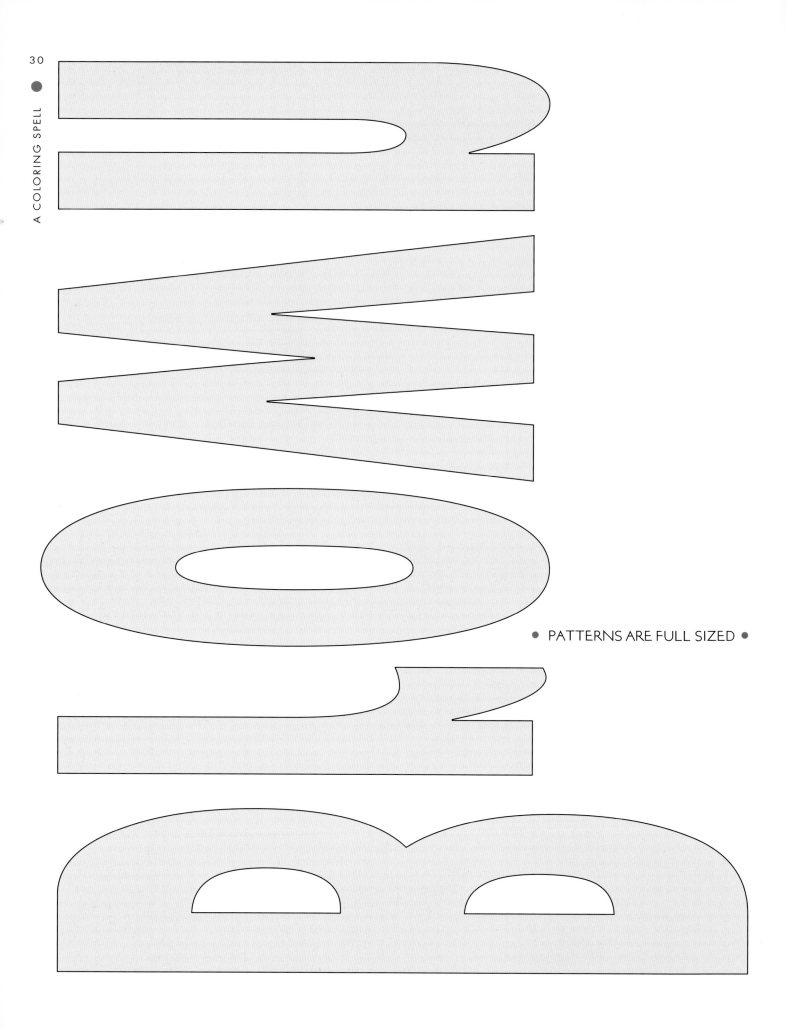

• PATTERNS ARE FULL SIZED •

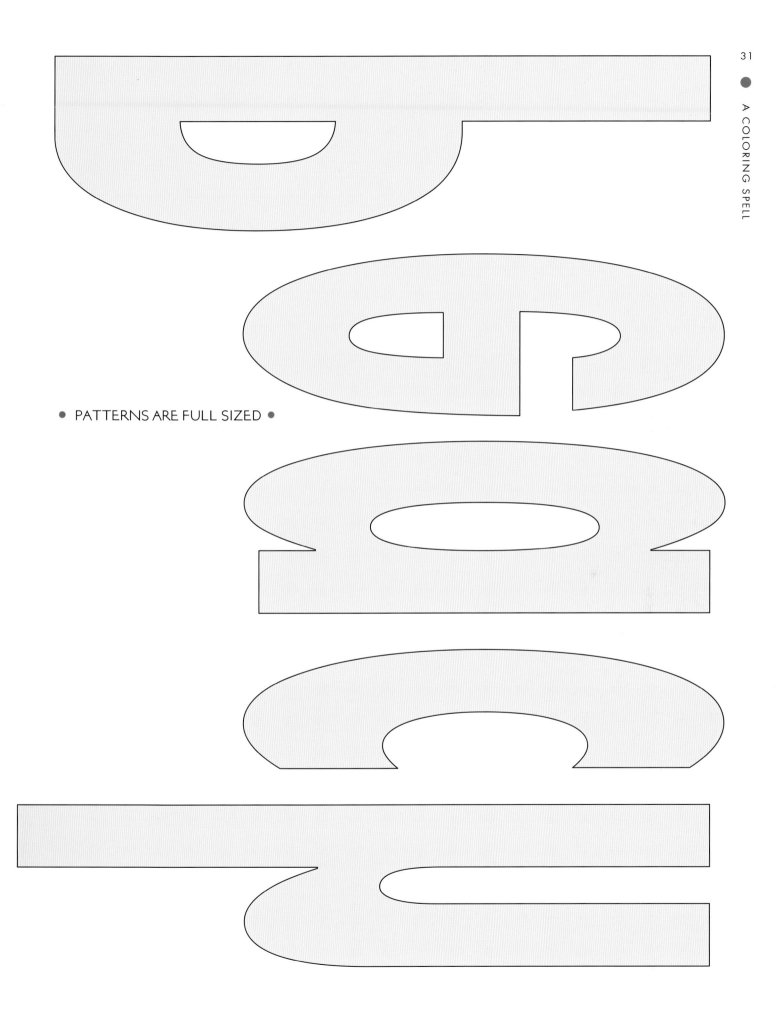

● PATTERNS ARE FULL SIZED ●

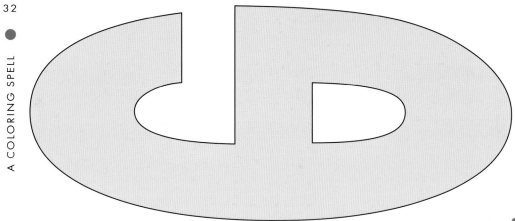

● PATTERNS ARE FULL SIZED ●

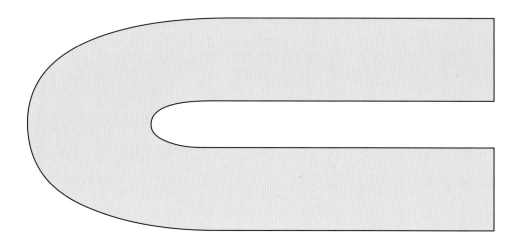

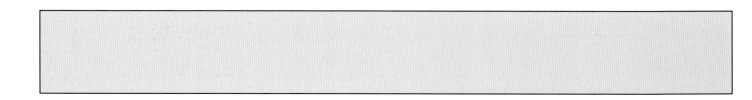

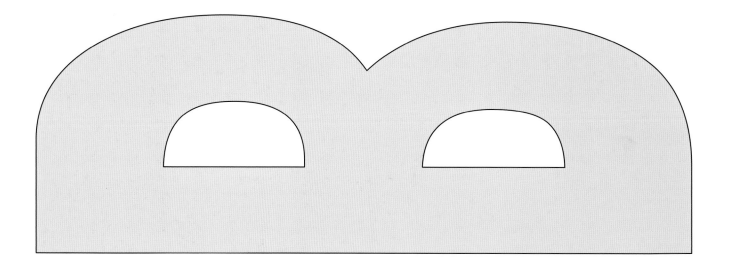

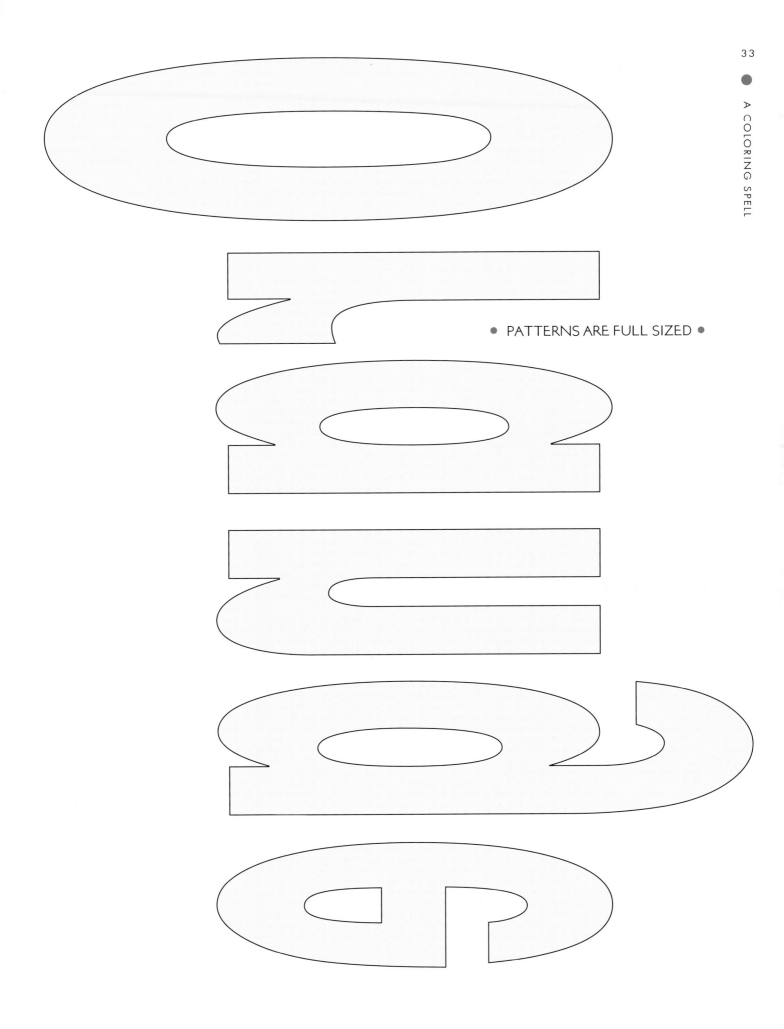

● PATTERNS ARE FULL SIZED ●

Hanna's Place Mat by Chris Lynn Kirsch

MY OWN **PLACE MAT**

All children feel important when they have possessions that are uniquely their own. Not only will this place mat make your child feel special, but it will help him or her learn to set the table correctly and spell the names of the items as they are put in place!

Finished Place Mat: 17" x 13½"

MATERIALS

Fat quarters measure approximately 18" x 21". Note that the backing fabric is folded over the finished place mat to bind the edges. If you prefer a different color scheme, be sure to choose two brightly colored fabrics that contrast well for the place mat top and a third high-contrast fabric for the backing.

Fat quarter of lime green tone-on-tone print for background and words

Fat quarter of medium purple tone-on-tone print for name and shapes

Fat quarter of dark purple tone-on-tone print for backing and rollover binding

13½" x 17" piece of thin cotton batting

CUTTING

Cut all pieces across the 21" fabric width.

From the medium purple tone-on-tone print, cut:
1 rectangle, 14" x 18"

From the lime green tone-on-tone print, cut:
1 rectangle, 14" x 18"

From the dark purple tone-on-tone print, cut:
1 rectangle, 16½" x 20"

MAKING THE PLACE MAT

I appliquéd this project using the repliqué method described on page 9 because the appliqué fabric can be layered on the background in one piece, eliminating the hassle of cutting and fusing multiple small pieces. Refer to "Appliqué Techniques" on page 8 for guidance as needed.

1. Photocopy or trace the full-sized patterns on pages 38–39 to create pattern sheets for the cup, napkin, fork, plate, knife, and spoon. Leave the plate-knife-and-spoon pattern whole, but cut the cup away from the napkin-and-fork portion of the pattern so you can position these elements properly on the place mat. Trim the excess paper ¼" outside the cup outline.

2. Refer to "Creating Patterns" on page 6 to make the pattern for your special child's name. *Be sure to print the text in reverse when creating your own patterns.* Make the name pattern no larger than a 3" x 10" rectangle so the name fits comfortably with the other pattern pieces. Trim the excess paper ¼" outside the name.

3. Place the 14" x 18" medium purple rectangle on your work surface wrong side up. Layer the 14" x 18" lime green background rectangle on top, again with the wrong side up. Pin the two rectangles together at the corners.

4. Arrange the patterns (including the name) on the wrong side of the lime green print as shown, leaving a 1" margin all the way around the perimeter of the place mat. Pin or tape the patterns in place.

Background fabric
(wrong side up)

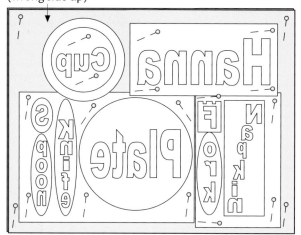

5. Refer to "Repliqué" on page 9 to stitch along the lines of all shapes and words, to trim away the appliqué fabric close to the stitching, and to finish the raw edges with satin stitching. Note that the shapes will appear in the appliqué fabric, while the words *inside* the shapes will appear in the background fabric.

FINISHING

For detailed instructions on finishing techniques, refer to "Finishing Basics" on page 69.

1. Remove the paper pattern from the wrong side of the place mat. Press well from the wrong side using spray starch and steam.

2. Trim the place mat to 13½" x 17".

3. Place the dark purple backing rectangle wrong side up. Center the batting over the backing, and then add the place mat right side up. Baste the layers together.

4. Hand or machine quilt as desired. I quilted around the letters and shapes. Then, since a quilted place mat will probably endure many washings, I heavily machine quilted the background with echo quilting and free-motion squiggles to make the mat more durable.

5. Steam press the entire place mat once again to ensure a flat finished project.

6. Rotary cut the backing fabric 1" away from the raw edges of the place mat top and batting as shown.

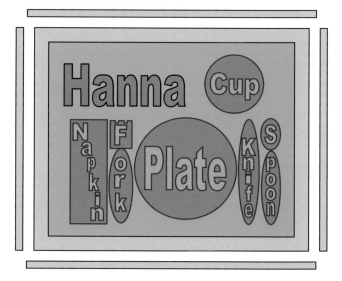

7. Starting along the bottom edge of the place mat, fold the raw edge of the backing fabric up to meet the raw edges of the place mat top and batting. Fold the backing edge up again, over the raw edge of the place mat and batting, to form a ½"-wide binding. Secure the binding with pins or binding clips.

Repeat along the entire bottom edge, continuing off the left edge of the place mat.

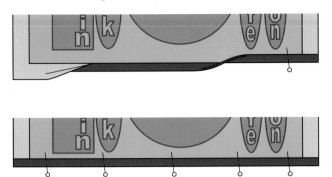

8. Fold the corner of the backing at a 45° angle so the bottom folded edge is now touching the raw edge on the left side of the place mat as shown.

9. Keeping this corner fold in place, double fold the backing on the left edge of the place mat as you did along the bottom edge. The angled fold you made in step 8 will fold to the top of the place mat in a perfect miter.

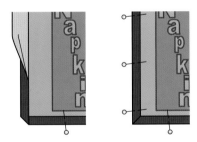

10. Continue around the remaining sides of the place mat, folding and pinning the rollover binding in place. Topstitch the binding using a straight or decorative machine stitch in a matching or contrasting thread color.

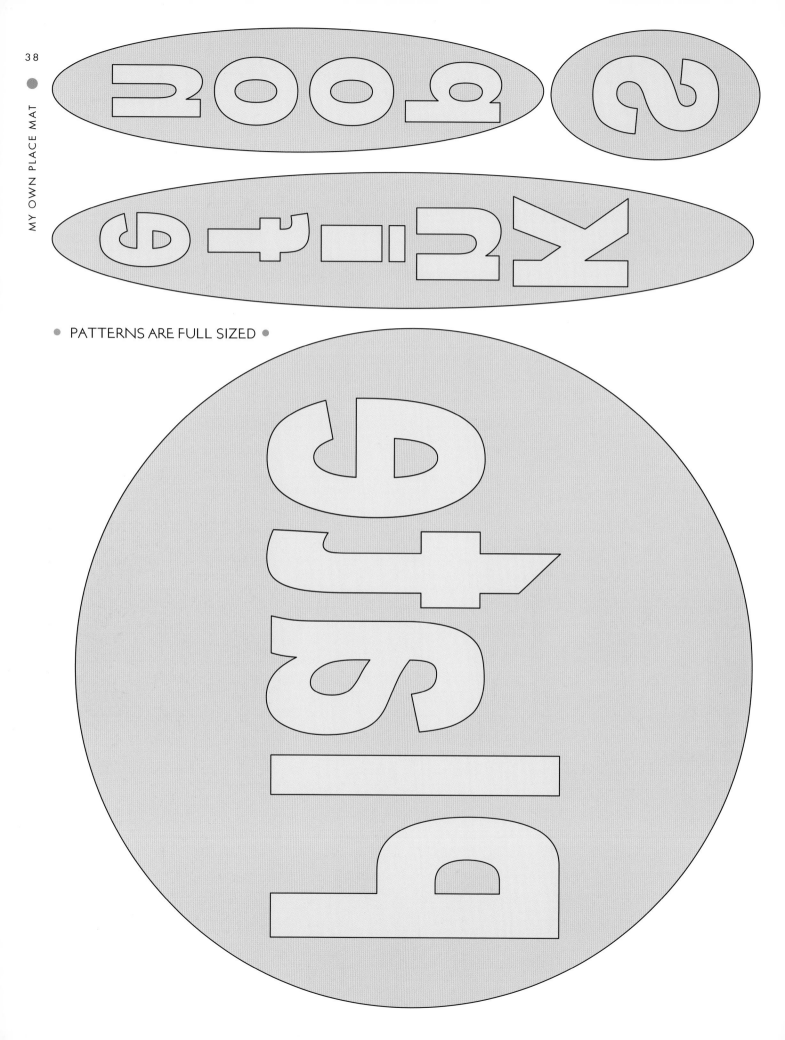

● PATTERNS ARE FULL SIZED ●

● PATTERNS ARE FULL SIZED ●

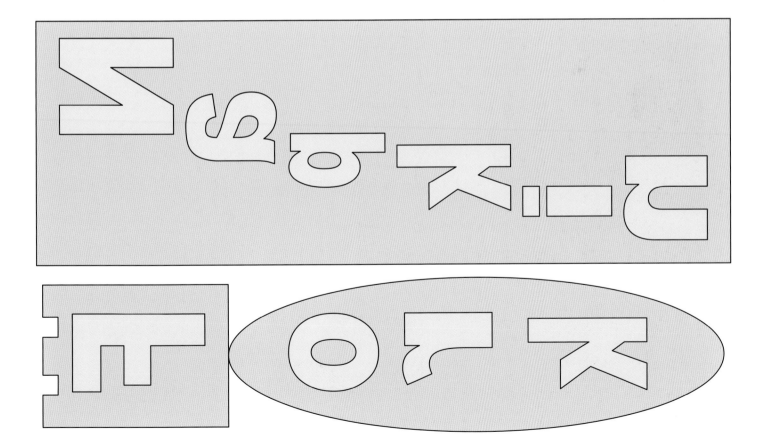

Touch Me, Feel Me, Read Me by Chris Lynn Kirsch

TOUCH ME, FEEL ME, READ ME

This quilt is all about textures and shapes, right down to the chenille loop-the-loops. These are great concepts for a child to learn and understand. The crop of fabrics available today makes this project an educational extravaganza. As you read the materials list, you'll find suggestions for selecting (or creating) just the right fabric, but feel free to do your own thing.

Finished Quilt: 37½" x 48½"

MATERIALS

Yardage is based on 42"-wide fabric. The background in the quilt shown on page 40 uses five different blue fabrics. Choose five different blues in a variety of values that work well together. Refer to the fabric placement diagram on page 42 for guidance. If you prefer a different color palette, choose background fabric that contrasts well with the "word" fabric so the words are easy to read.

⅞ yard of blue fabric 1 (B1) for background

⅜ yard of blue fabric 2 (B2) for background

½ yard of blue fabric 3 (B3) for background

½ yard of blue fabric 4 (B4) for background

½ yard of blue fabric 5 (B5) for background

10" x 10" square of yellow polka-dot cotton fabric for *Round*

10" x 10" square of yellow plaid cotton fabric for *Square*

9" x 12" rectangle of yellow cotton flannel for *Soft*

9" x 12" rectangle of yellow polar fleece for *Fluffy*

9" x 12" rectangle of yellow cotton fabric for *Rough**

9" x 12" rectangle of yellow cotton fabric for *Smooth**

9" x 12" rectangle of yellow cotton fabric for *Thick*

8" x 12" rectangle of yellow cotton fabric for *Bumpy**

8" x 12" rectangle of gold tricot lamé for *Shiny*

4" x 12" rectangle of yellow cotton fabric for *Thin*

½ yard of yellow fabric for binding

2⅓ yards of fabric for backing with horizontal seam **or** 3 yards of fabric for backing with vertical seam

42" x 53" piece of batting

9" x 12" rectangle of coarse netting for *Rough* (optional)*

9" x 12" rectangle of clear plastic or vinyl for *Smooth* (optional)*

8 yards of yellow chenille-by-the-inch (or rickrack) for embellishment

*See the box on page 42 for tips on creating your own bumpy, smooth, and rough fabric. To make your own bumpy fabric, you will need a 12" x 15" rectangle.

Creating Your Own *Bumpy, Smooth,* and *Rough* Fabric

If you can't find the perfect fabric for these words, create your own as I did.

Bumpy Fabric

1. Wet a 12" x 15" rectangle of cotton fabric. Pleat, fold, and roll it into a lumpy snake.

2. Twist the snake tightly and fold it onto itself.

3. Secure with a rubber band and let dry. (Throwing it in the dryer will speed up the process.)

4. Remove the rubber band and unroll the fabric on an ironing surface, stretching and flattening until the piece is just bumpy enough.

5. Using a steam iron on the cotton setting, press straight down on the manipulated fabric to press the bumps in place, cut the piece to measure 8" x 12", and then set aside until you're ready to appliqué.

Smooth and *Rough* Fabric

I used 9" x 12" rectangles of the same cotton fabric for both *Smooth* and *Rough*. I covered the *Smooth* rectangle with a piece of clear plastic (sold in the oilcloth section of the fabric store) and covered the *Rough* rectangle with a rectangle of coarse netting.

CUTTING

Cut all strips across the fabric width.

From blue fabric 1 (B1), cut:
1 rectangle, 13½" x 37½", for piece B1a
1 square, 12½" x 12½", for piece B1c
1 rectangle, 8½" x 18½", for piece B1b

From blue fabric 2 (B2), cut:
1 rectangle, 5½" x 37½", for piece B2a
1 rectangle, 5½" x 17½", for piece B2b

From blue fabric 3 (B3), cut:
1 rectangle, 12½" x 18½"

From blue fabric 4 (B4), cut:
1 rectangle, 13½" x 17½", for piece B4a
1 rectangle, 6½" x 12½", for piece B4b

From blue fabric 5 (B5), cut:
1 rectangle, 12½" x 31½"

From the yellow fabric for binding, cut:
5 strips, 2½" x 42"

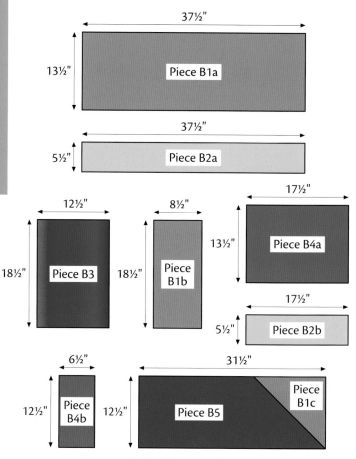

Fabric placement diagram

MAKING THE BLOCKS

I appliquéd this project using the reverse-repliqué method described on page 10, because I find it the best option for working with unusual (noncotton) and specialty fabric. Create pattern sheets for each of the 10 words by photocopying or tracing the full-sized patterns on pages 46–55.

Soft, Bumpy, and Fluffy Block

1. Place the B1a rectangle wrong side up and horizontally on your work surface.

2. Place the 9" x 12" *Soft* rectangle wrong side up on the B1a rectangle, 1½" from the upper-right corner.

3. Place the *Soft* pattern right side up on the wrong side of the *Soft* rectangle. Pin through all layers and use the reverse-repliqué technique described on page 10 to create the word.

4. Place the 9" x 12" *Fluffy* rectangle wrong side up on the wrong side of the B1a rectangle, 1½" from the upper-left corner. Follow step 3 using the *Fluffy* pattern to create the word.

5. Place the 8" x 12" *Bumpy* rectangle wrong side up on the wrong side of the B1a rectangle, centering the *Bumpy* rectangle 1½" from the bottom edge of B1a. Follow step 3 using the *Bumpy* pattern to create the word.

Reduce the Bulk!

Since the polar fleece, layered fabric, and manipulated fabric can be bulky, tear away the paper pattern after satin stitching and trim the excess fabric to ¼" from the stitching.

Rough and Smooth Block

1. Place the B3 rectangle wrong side up and vertically on your work surface.

2. Place the 9" x 12" *Rough* rectangle wrong side up on the B3 rectangle, near the top and angled downward from the upper right. If you are using netting as described in the box on page 42, slip the 9" x 12" piece of netting between the B3 rectangle and the *Rough* rectangle.

3. Place the *Rough* pattern right side up on the wrong side of the *Rough* rectangle. Pin through all layers and use the reverse-repliqué technique described on page 10 to create the word. Be careful not to cut the netting when trimming away the background fabric.

4. Repeat steps 2 and 3, substituting the 9" x 12" *Smooth* rectangle for the *Rough* rectangle and substituting the 9" x 12" rectangle of plastic (or vinyl) for the netting. Position them, along with the *Smooth* pattern, near the bottom on the wrong side of the B3 rectangle. Angle the fabric, plastic, and pattern upward from the lower right.

Satin Stitching on Plastic

The feed dogs and presser-foot runners tend to bog down and stick when used for stitching on plastic. To counteract the drag, place the edge of an index card under the side of the presser foot that touches the plastic and continue to pivot and rotate the card to keep it under the foot while stitching. This should keep things moving smoothly.

Thin and Thick Block

1. Place the B4a rectangle wrong side up and horizontally on your work surface.

2. Place the 4" x 12" *Thin* rectangle wrong side up on the B4a rectangle at an equal distance from the top, bottom, and right edges.

3. Place the *Thin* pattern right side up on the wrong side of the *Thin* rectangle. Pin through all layers and use the reverse-repliqué technique described on page 10 to create the word.

4. Place the 9" x 12" *Thick* rectangle wrong side up on the wrong side of the B4a rectangle, 1½" from the left edge and centered top to bottom. Follow step 3, using the *Thick* pattern to stitch the word in place.

Round and Square Block

The outlines for *Round* and *Square* will be added during the embellishing step.

1. Place the B5 rectangle wrong side up and horizontally on your work surface.

2. Place the 10" *Round* square wrong side up on the B5 rectangle, 1" from the top and right edges.

3. Place the *Round* pattern right side up on the wrong side of the *Round* square. Pin through all layers and use the reverse-repliqué technique described on page 10 to create the word.

4. Place the 10" *Square* square wrong side up on the wrong side of the B5 rectangle, 3" to the left of the word *Round* and 1" from the bottom of the B5 rectangle. Follow step 3 using the *Square* pattern to create the word.

Shiny Block

1. Press the B1c square in half diagonally, wrong sides together.

2. Open the square and orient it wrong side up so the diagonal crease runs from the upper left to the lower right. Place the 8" x 12" *Shiny* rectangle wrong side up on the wrong side of the B5 square, in the lower triangle, aligning a long edge of the *Shiny* rectangle with the diagonal crease.

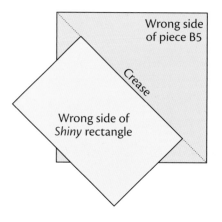

Wrong side of piece B5

Crease

Wrong side of *Shiny* rectangle

3. Place the *Shiny* pattern right side up on the wrong side of the *Shiny* rectangle, with the top of the word facing the lower-left corner of the square. Pin through all layers and use the reverse-repliqué technique described on page 10 to create the word.

Joining B1c to B5

This sew-and-flip technique is a great way to add corners (right-angle triangles) to squares and rectangles without having to deal with bias edges.

1. Place the B5 unit on your work surface right side up.

2. With right sides together and raw edges aligned, place the B1c *(Shiny)* square in the upper-right corner of the B5 *(Round/Square)* unit. Make sure the diagonal crease runs from upper left to lower right and the word *Shiny* is in the lower triangle. Straight stitch directly on the crease.

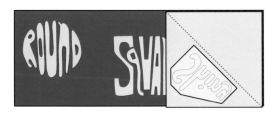

3. Fold the lower triangle back toward the upper-right corner and hand or machine baste around the corner to secure.

PUTTING IT TOGETHER

Part of what makes this quilt so interesting is the many oddly shaped blocks. To avoid frustration when stitching the blocks together, assemble the blocks in the order described below. Begin by arranging the blocks as shown in the fabric placement diagram on page 42 and proceed as follows:

1. Sew B2a to the bottom of B1a. Press the seam allowances toward B2a.

2. Sew B1b to the right edge of B3. Press the seam allowances toward B1b.

3. Sew B2b to the bottom of B4a. Press the seam allowances toward B2b.

4. Sew the unit from step 2 to the left edge of the unit from step 3. Press the seam allowances toward the step 2 unit.

5. Sew B4b to the left edge of the B5-and-B1c unit. Press the seam allowances toward B4b.

6. Sew the units from steps 1, 4, and 5 together. Press the seam allowances toward the top edge of the quilt.

Assembly diagram

FINISHING

For detailed instructions on finishing techniques, refer to "Finishing Basics" on page 69.

1. Refer to the quilt photo on page 40. Using a removable marker, determine where the loop-the-loop embellishments will go and draw this line on the quilt top. Draw a circle around the word *Round* and a square around the word *Square* for embellishing also.

2. Piece the backing, and then layer the backing, batting, and quilt top. Baste the layers together.

3. Using a walking foot, machine stitch the chenille-by-the-inch (or rickrack) along the lines you marked in step 1.

4. Machine or hand quilt as desired. I free-motion quilted around the words and loops, filling in the background areas with spirals and other meandering designs.

5. Straighten the sides and square up the corners of the quilt sandwich, trimming the batting and backing even with the quilt top.

6. Use the 2½"-wide yellow strips to make and attach a binding to the quilt.

7. Add a label to your quilt.

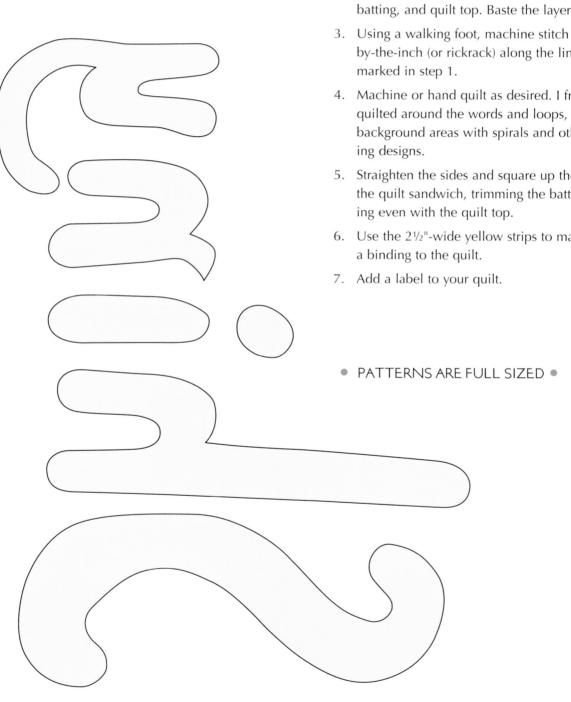

● PATTERNS ARE FULL SIZED ●

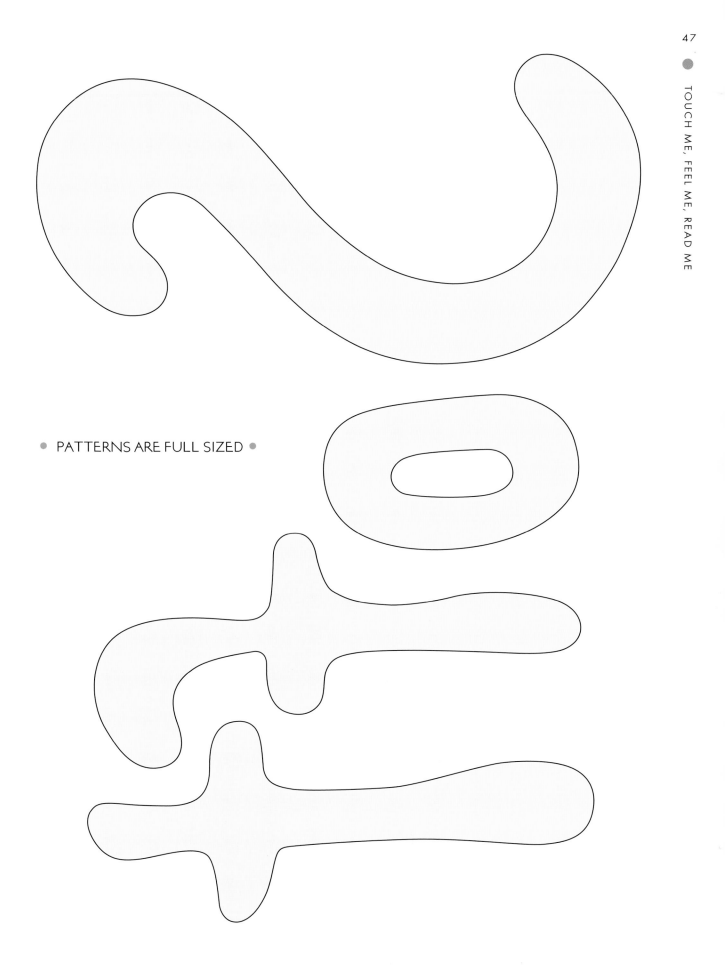

PATTERNS ARE FULL SIZED

● PATTERNS ARE FULL SIZED ●

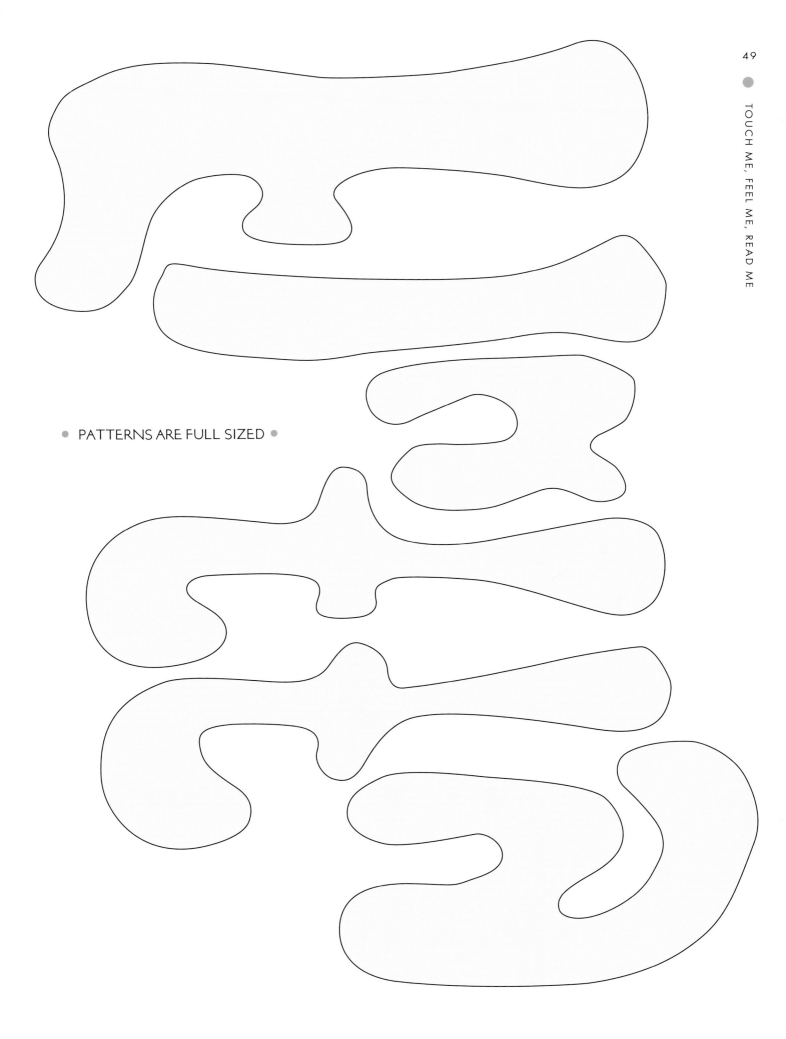

● PATTERNS ARE FULL SIZED ●

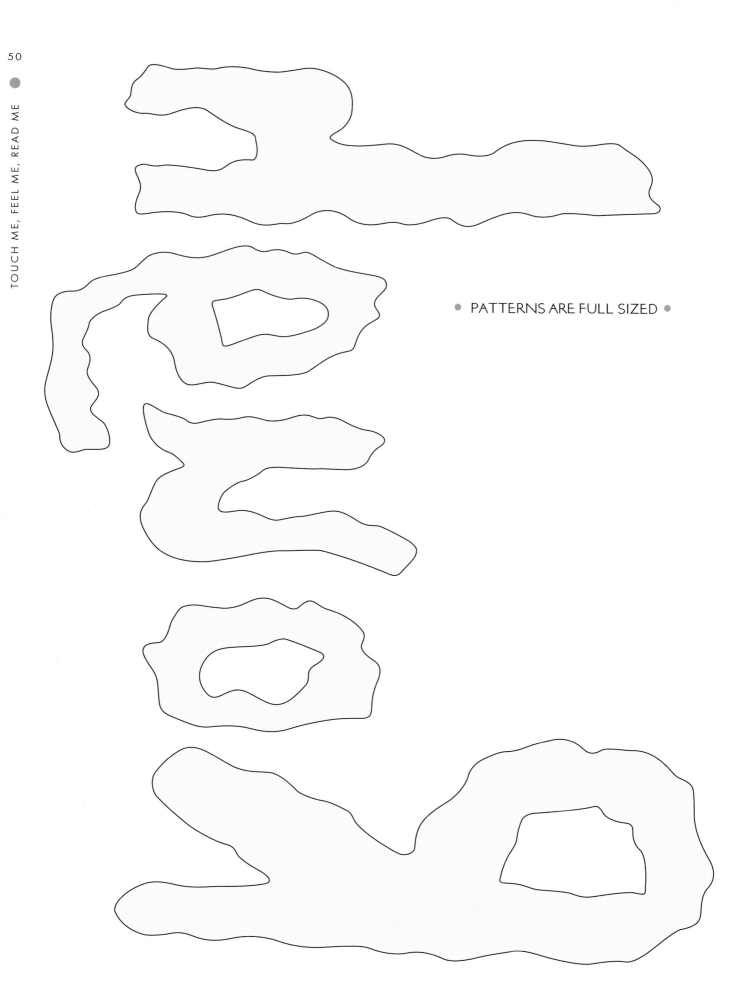

● PATTERNS ARE FULL SIZED ●

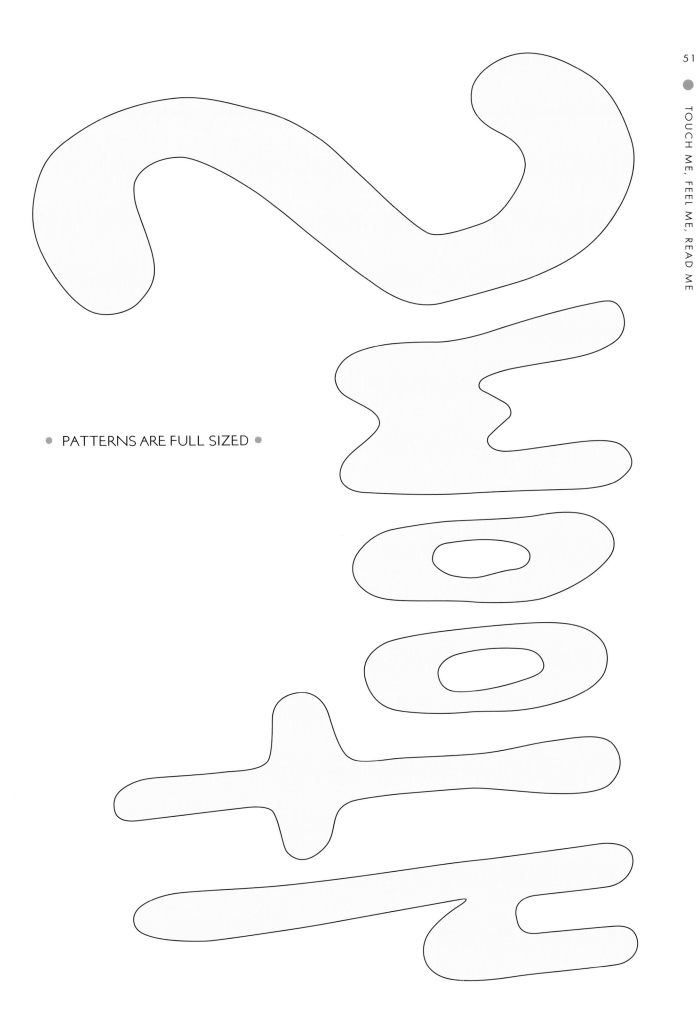

PATTERNS ARE FULL SIZED

PATTERNS ARE FULL SIZED

● PATTERNS ARE FULL SIZED ●

PATTERNS ARE FULL SIZED

Counting on Buttons by Chris Lynn Kirsch

COUNTING ON BUTTONS

This bright and appealing quilt uses many of the fun, colorful buttons available at craft and sewing stores. Choose good-quality buttons! They will be stitched on very securely, but be aware of the choking danger with infants and toddlers, and make this special project for a child of an appropriate age.

Have fun choosing the nine different button groups. Perhaps your special child will want to be in on the adventure of finding just the right ones. Of course, you will need to purchase the appropriate number of buttons for each square (one button for square 1, two buttons for square 2, and so on).

The words in each block are created in machine quilting. In order to stitch them in a continuous line, I've used cursive writing. A child who's learned cursive in school will be able to read the words, so that's another reason to make this project for an older child.

Finished Quilt: 43½" x 43½" ● Finished Block: 9" x 9"

MATERIALS

Yardage is based on 42"-wide fabric. Choose two high-contrast solid fabrics for the alternating background squares and one additional contrasting solid for the numbers.

⅞ yard of red solid for background squares and border corners

⅞ yard of purple tone-on-tone print for inner border and binding

⅞ yard of coordinating striped fabric for outer border*

⅔ yard of yellow solid for alternating background squares

⅝ yard of blue solid for numbers

2¾ yards of fabric for backing

48" x 48" piece of batting

9 groups of assorted whimsical buttons (group 1 has 1 button, group 2 has 2 buttons, etc.)

Beading thread

Water-erasable marker

Large-eyed needle

1¼ yards of 18"-wide paper-backed fusible web (not required for repliqué technique)

This yardage is sufficient for fabric with stripes that run either parallel to the selvage or from selvage to selvage.

CUTTING

Cut all strips across the fabric width unless noted otherwise.

From the red solid, cut:

2 strips, 10" x 42"; crosscut into 5 squares, 10" x 10"

1 strip, 6" x 42"; crosscut into 4 squares, 6" x 6"

From the yellow solid, cut:

2 strips, 10" x 42"; crosscut into 4 squares, 10" x 10"

From the blue solid, cut:

2 strips, 8" x 42"; crosscut into 9 squares, 8" x 8"*

From the purple tone-on-tone print, cut:

2 strips, 3" x 27½"

2 strips, 3" x 32½"

5 binding strips, 2½" x 42"

From the *lengthwise grain* of the coordinating striped fabric (for stripes that run parallel to the selvage), cut:**

4 strips, 6" x 32½"

*Cut these squares for the repliqué method only. For paper-backed fusible appliqué, you will cut the numbers individually.

**For fabric with stripes that run from selvage to selvage, cut these strips across the width of the fabric.

MAKING THE BLOCKS

Refer to "Appliqué Techniques" on page 8 for guidance as needed.

1. Photocopy or trace the full-sized number patterns on pages 61–63 for numbers 1–9 to create pattern sheets for repliqué, or trace the numbers on fusible web for paper-backed fusible appliqué. (I've given you the number 0 as well so you'll have a complete set for future use.)

2. Use either the paper-backed fusible appliqué method or the repliqué method to create each number on its 10" red or yellow background square. Appliqué odd numbers on the red background squares and even numbers on the yellow squares. If you're using the repliqué method, remove the paper pattern from the wrong side of each block. If you are using the paper-backed fusible appliqué method, remove any stabilizer.

3. Press each block well from the wrong side using spray starch and steam.

4. Square up each block to 9½" x 9½", making sure each number remains centered in the background block.

PUTTING IT TOGETHER

1. Arrange the blocks in three horizontal rows of three blocks each as shown below.

2. Sew the blocks into horizontal rows; press. Sew the rows together to complete the quilt center— a large Nine Patch block.

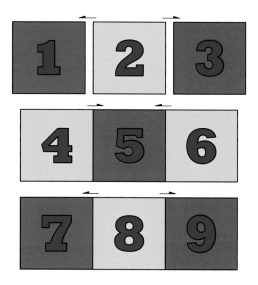

3. Square up the quilt top in preparation for borders. Sew the 3" x 27½" purple inner-border strips to the sides of the quilt. Press the seam allowances toward the border strips. Sew the 3" x 32½" purple inner-border strips to the top and bottom; press.

4. Sew two 6" x 32½" striped outer-border strips to the sides of the quilt. Press the seam allowances toward the newly added border strips. Sew a 6" red square to each end of each remaining 6" x 32½" striped outer-border strip. Press the seam allowances toward the border strips and sew these border strips to the top and bottom; press.

FINISHING

For detailed instructions on finishing techniques, refer to "Finishing Basics" on page 69.

1. Piece the backing, and then layer the backing, batting, and quilt top. Baste the layers together.

2. Hand or machine quilt as desired. I chose to quilt two words in each block: the name of the number and the name of the item depicted on the button. (For detailed instructions, refer to "Quilting Words" on page 60.) Using the walking foot on my machine, I stitched in the ditch between the blocks, and then I free-motion quilted around each number. I straight-stitched between the stripes in the outer border and added free-motion spirals in the corner squares.

3. Place the appropriate buttons in each block as desired. Hand stitch them in place *securely* using strong beading thread (available in bead stores) in a color that complements the buttons. Tie off each button with a double knot.

4. Square up the quilt sandwich, trimming the batting and backing even with the quilt top.

5. Use the 2½"-wide purple strips to make and attach a binding to the quilt.

6. Add a label to your quilt.

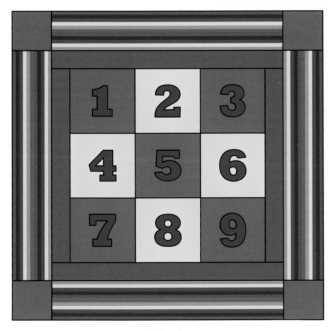

Quilt plan

Quilting Words

Writing the words in your own handwriting makes the quilt more meaningful. If you have never liked your penmanship—practice, practice, practice! If it helps you keep things straight and even, draw lines on the block with a ruler and an erasable marking tool before you begin.

1. Use the water-erasable marker to write the desired words on the front side of the block.

2. Thread your sewing machine (top and bobbin) in a thread color to match the background fabric, drop or cover the feed dogs, attach the darning or free-motion foot, and free-motion stitch along the written words.

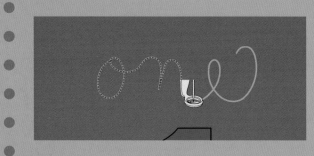

3. Place a mediumweight black thread in the top of the machine and a heavyweight black thread—such as size 5 pearl cotton—in the bobbin.

4. Turn the quilt over to the back; the stitched words will appear in reverse. Pull the bobbin thread to the surface, hold both thread tails, and begin free-motion quilting the word along the previous stitching.

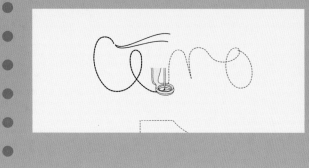

5. When you reach the end of the word, leave a minimum 4"-long tail of both top and bobbin thread. Turn the quilt over to the right side. Thread the thick thread into a large-eyed needle and pull this thread through to the back.

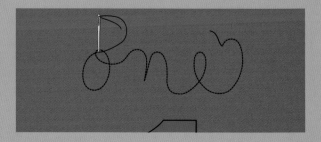

6. Tie the two starting thread tails into a square knot. To hide the tails, thread both onto the large-eyed needle and pull them between the quilt layers, exiting about 1" from your insertion point. Carefully clip the excess thread close to the quilt back. Repeat for the ending thread tails.

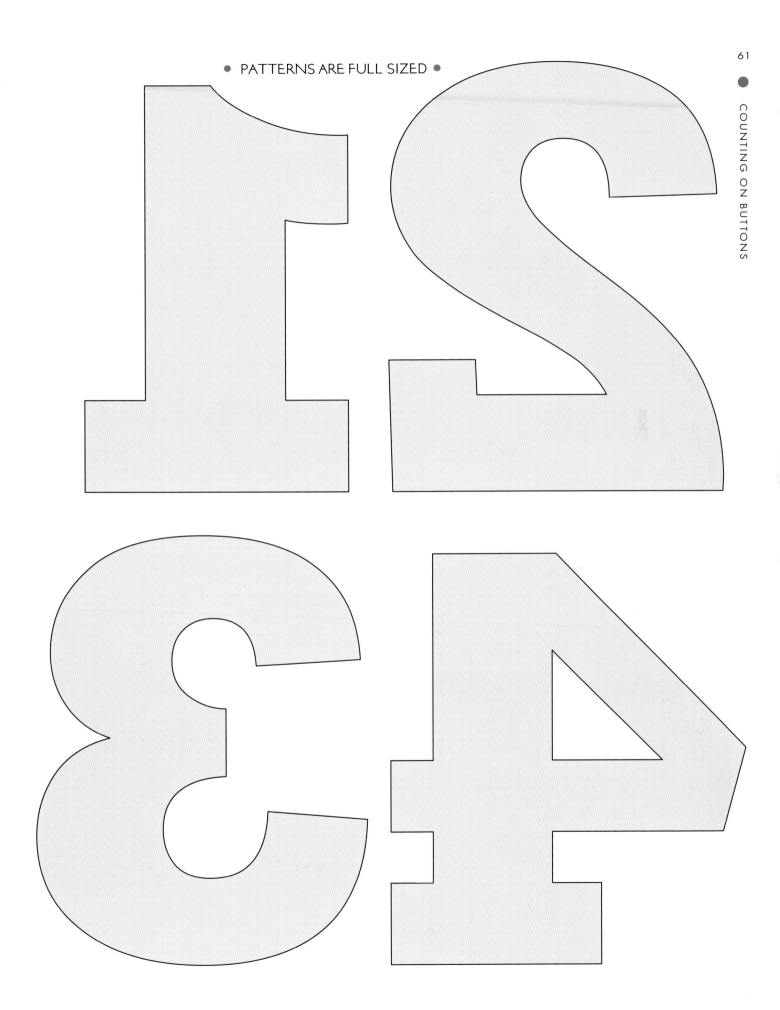

● PATTERNS ARE FULL SIZED ●

Kade's Rolled-Up Fun by Chris Lynn Kirsch

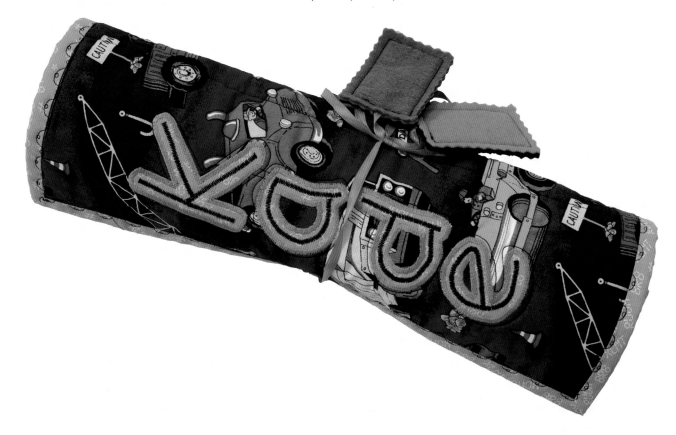

ROLLED-UP FUN

How unique: a carry-along toy to keep kids entertained that doesn't require batteries! This portable roll-up chalkboard is fun to make and can be personalized to fit your little learner's special interests. My nephew, Kade, loves trucks and construction equipment, so I searched for the perfect theme fabric and chose other fabrics to match. I found the chalkboard fabric at my local quilt shop. If you can't find it in your area, you can order it online from NancysNotions.com.

Finished Size: 23½" x 16"

MATERIALS

Yardage is based on 42"-wide fabric.

⅝ yard of theme fabric for right-edge border and backing

⅝ yard of contrasting fabric for child's name, chalkboard frame, and binding

10" x 12" rectangle of chalkboard fabric

16" x 23½" piece of thin cotton batting

6" piece of ¾"-wide black elastic for chalk loops

3" x 4" rectangle *each* of 3 different colors of felt for erasers

1 yard of ¼"-diameter cord or ¼"-wide ribbon for tie

¼ yard of 18"-wide paper-backed fusible web (not required for repliqué technique)

Pinking shears or rotary cutter with wavy blade

3 pieces of chalk

CUTTING

Cut all strips across the fabric width unless noted otherwise.

From the theme fabric, cut:
1 rectangle, 16" x 23½"

1 rectangle, 6" x 16"*

From the contrasting fabric, cut:
2 strips, 3½" x 42"; crosscut into:

   2 strips, 3½" x 12"

   2 strips, 3½" x 16"

1 strip, 4" x 16"**

3 strips, 2½" x 42"

*If this fabric has a directional motif that runs parallel to the selvage, cut this rectangle on the lengthwise grain of the fabric.

**Cut this strip for the repliqué method only. For paper-backed fusible appliqué, you will cut the letters individually.

Care of Chalkboard Fabric

Read and follow the instructions for your chalkboard fabric carefully. Special directives might include:

1. Avoid touching the fabric surface with a hot iron.

2. Cure the surface by rubbing it with chalk. Wash off the chalk and repeat.

3. If the fabric feeds poorly through your machine, stitch with paper over the surface. Remove the paper after stitching.

MAKING THE CHALKBOARD TOP

1. Sew the 3½" x 12" strips of contrasting fabric to the top and bottom of the 10" x 12" chalkboard rectangle as shown; press. Sew the 3½" x 16" strips of contrasting fabric to the sides; press.

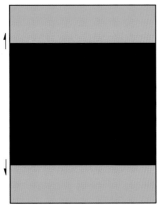

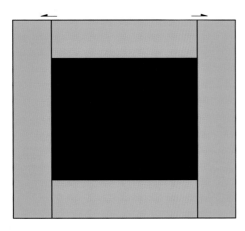

2. Cut the elastic into three pieces, 2" long. Fold each piece in half and, with raw edges even, place them along the right edge of the framed chalkboard as shown. Secure each with a pin.

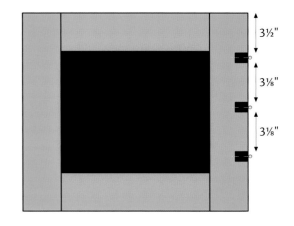

3. Pin the 6" x 16" theme-fabric rectangle right sides together with the unit from step 2 as shown, capturing the raw edges of the elastic between the layers. Sew the pieces together. Press the seam allowance away from the loops.

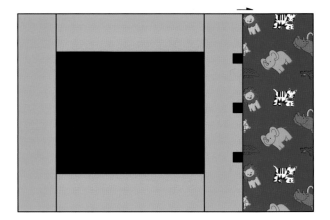

4. Place a piece of chalk in each loop. If the loops are too large, topstitch ⅛" to ¼" from the seam to shorten the loops. (This will also stabilize the loops.) Remove the chalk for now.

ADDING THE NAME

Refer to "Appliqué Techniques" on page 8 for guidance as needed to add the child's name to the back of the chalkboard.

1. Refer to "Creating Patterns" on page 6 to make the pattern sheet (for repliqué) or letter patterns (for paper-backed fusible appliqué) for your child's name. For repliqué, print the name using the portrait orientation for the paper and write the name vertically, top to bottom. *Be sure to print the text in reverse when creating your own patterns.*

2. If you're using the fusible method, prepare and fuse the letters 1¾" from the left edge on the right side of the 16" x 23½" rectangle of theme fabric. Remove any stabilizer, and then read "Bump Up the Contrast" at right and proceed to "Finishing" on page 68.

3. If you are using the repliqué method, place the 16" x 23½" rectangle of theme fabric right side up on your work surface.

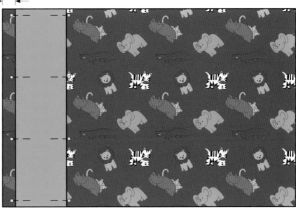

4. Place the 4" x 16" strip of contrasting fabric right side up and vertically, 1½" from the left edge of the theme fabric. Pin in place.

5. Turn the unit from step 4 over so the wrong side of the backing fabric faces you. Center the pattern right side up and vertically, 1½" from the right edge of the background fabric, secure it with pins or transparent tape, and then hold the unit up to the light to check that the pattern and the contrasting fabric are aligned.

6. Use the repliqué method to create the name.

7. Remove the paper pattern and press well from the wrong side using spray starch and steam.

Bump Up the Contrast

My orange fabric was bright, but because the backing fabric was so busy, the letters didn't stand out as much as I would have liked. I decided to satin stitch in black thread down the center of each letter to emphasize the child's name. Another alternative would have been to appliqué an orange rectangle in place first and then appliqué the letters onto this rectangle in black.

Note how the black satin stitching makes the letters of Kade's name more prominent against the busy theme fabric.

FINISHING

For detailed instructions on finishing techniques, refer to "Finishing Basics" on page 69.

1. Layer the backing wrong side up on your work surface. (The wrong side of the name appliqué will be to the right).

2. Layer the batting rectangle on the backing, and then layer the chalkboard unit right side up on the batting.

3. Avoiding the chalkboard fabric, baste through all the layers using safety pins.

4. Hand or machine quilt as desired. I used thread to match the contrasting fabric and machine quilted ⅛" outside the perimeter of the chalkboard fabric and ⅛" from the seam holding the elastic loops. This anchored the seam allowances underneath. Using the same thread, I made a line of stitching 1" above the top edge of the chalkboard and 1¾" below the bottom edge. I used these lines as a base to free-motion quilt the alphabet in black thread. If you wish, you can add numbers to the side borders. I finished by stitching around the name on the reverse side with free-motion quilting.

5. Square up the quilt sandwich.

6. Place the quilted unit on the work surface, backing side up. Fold the piece of cording or ribbon in half lengthwise, and place the fold, centered vertically, along the raw edge of the quilt, next to the name. Pin in place.

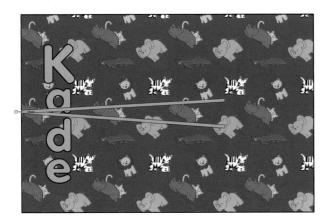

7. Use the 2½"-wide contrasting strips to make and attach a binding. Finish the binding with your choice of decorative stitch.

MAKING THE ERASERS

For extra whimsy, I added a felt eraser to each end of the tie. I made mine rectangles, but they could easily be made in a shape to match the quilt. Ideas for shapes can be gleaned from simple cookie cutters, coloring book drawings, or your imagination.

1. Cut two 2" x 3" rectangles or other shapes from each piece of felt.

2. Layer three pieces of felt (one of each color) and stitch around the perimeter of the shape, ¼" from the edge, leaving a ½" opening to insert the tie. Trim the edges with a rotary cutter equipped with a wavy blade or with pinking shears. Make two.

3. Slip one end of the tie ½" into the opening of each eraser. Sew the opening shut to secure the tie.

4. Reinsert the chalk into the loops and roll the quilt up, backing side out, starting from the edge without the name. "Rolled-Up Fun" is now ready to be given to a special child.

This chapter covers the finishing techniques required to turn each project into a quilt: layering, quilting, binding, adding a label, and more. Remember: each project is different and these are only guidelines to follow. It is up to you to add the special touches that make your quilt unique.

LAYERING AND BASTING THE QUILT SANDWICH

After the paper (or stabilizer) has been removed from the back of the quilt top, the top is ready for layering with batting and backing. These pieces should be cut at least 2" larger than the quilt top on all sides.

1. Spread the pressed backing wrong side up on a clean, flat work surface. Secure the backing with masking tape in several places along the edges to keep it smooth and taut.

2. Smooth the batting over the backing, and then center the quilt top over the batting right side up.

3. Beginning at the center of the quilt, baste the layers together with safety pins spaced about 3" apart. I prefer size 1 safety pins because they make smaller holes in the fabric.

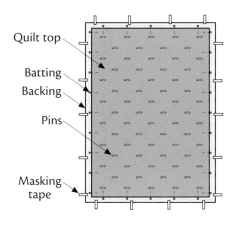

Quilt top

Batting

Backing

Pins

Masking tape

QUILTING

Snuggle-and-Learn quilts require simple quilting to hold the layers together—the appliqués are the focal feature. Free-motion machine quilting works well around the letters and numbers; however, the addition of fun, free-motion swirls and loops in the block backgrounds can add whimsy and durability to the quilt. The more quilting on a project, the better it will wash and wear.

Hand quilting would also be a delightful way to finish one of these projects. Traditionally, hand stitches should be small and even, but Snuggle-and-Learn quilts are not your traditional type of quilt. The big-stitch technique is quite popular and adds a nice touch because the stitches are larger (⅛"–¼") and can be done in bright colors with thicker thread, thus bringing additional texture and excitement to the quilt. Big stitches look best if the stitch and the space between are of equal length.

However you choose to hold the layers of your quilt together, be sure it is a technique you enjoy, so the whole process is fun. Some individualized suggestions are included with each project, but please feel free to let your creativity take over.

ADDING A HANGING SLEEVE

Many of these quilts look good hanging on the wall between snuggles. A thin (½"-diameter) dowel slides easily into the sleeve described below and supports the entire quilt well without being visible from the front. By leaving an opening at the center of the sleeve, you can easily hang a small quilt on a single nail. On a larger quilt, use a nail at each end of the dowel plus one in the center. (The center nail eliminates sagging.) I prefer to add the sleeve before attaching the binding to the quilt.

1. Cut a strip of fabric with a width of 4" and a length that matches the width of the quilt minus 1".

2. Cut the strip in half across its width. Turn under ¼" along each short end and machine topstitch in place.

3. Square up the quilt by trimming the batting and backing even with the edges of the quilt top, making sure the corners are square. Pin through all three layers along the outer edge at 2" intervals.

4. Fold the hemmed sleeve strips in half lengthwise, wrong sides together. Align the long raw edges with the top edge of the quilt, leaving a ½" gap between the sleeves. Pin the sleeves in place.

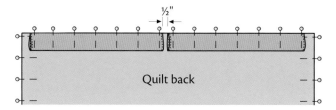

½"

Quilt back

5. Bind the quilt as described below. The top edges of the sleeves will be caught in the binding; hand stitch the bottom edges of the sleeves to the quilt back with a blind stitch and matching thread, making sure the stitches do not go through to the front of the quilt.

BINDING

There are many, many ways to bind a quilt, and I think I have tried them all. The following method is a combination of my favorite techniques. I think it gives a wonderful finished edge to the quilt.

1. Cut enough 2½" strips across the width of the binding fabric to go around the outside of the quilt, plus at least 10" to allow for joining strips and turning corners. Join the strips with diagonal seams as shown to make one long strip. Press the seam allowances open to reduce the bulk.

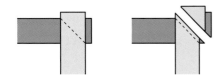

2. Position the binding around the outside edge of the quilt and rearrange the binding so that no seams fall at the quilt corners. When you are satisfied with the placement, place the beginning of the binding strip on the quilt top with right sides together, aligning the raw edge of the binding with the raw edge of the quilt.

3. Start 8" from the beginning of the binding strip with a backstitch, and use a ½" seam allowance and a walking foot to stitch the binding to the quilt. Stop ½" from the corner; backstitch and remove the quilt from the machine.

4. Fold the binding strip up so the fold creates a 45° angle.

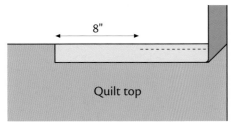

8"

Quilt top

5. Fold the binding down over the angled fold to create a second fold even with the upper edge of the quilt. The raw edges of the binding should be even with the raw edges on the adjacent side of the quilt; pin.

6. Begin stitching at the edge of the quilt and continue stitching the binding to the quilt with a ½" seam, turning each corner as you come to it in the manner described in steps 4 and 5. Stop stitching 8" from the point where you originally began stitching the binding to the quilt.

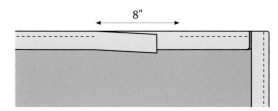

8"

7. Cut *only* the end tail at a 45° angle halfway between the beginning and ending stitching.

8. Place the trimmed end tail over the beginning tail and draw the 45° angle on the beginning tail.

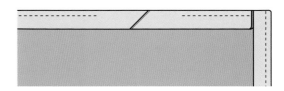

9. Lift the end tail and cut the beginning tail ½" to the left of the drawn line.

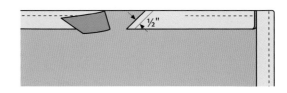

½"

10. Lift the binding up off the quilt and place the ends right sides together as shown. Stitch the ends together using a ¼" seam allowance.

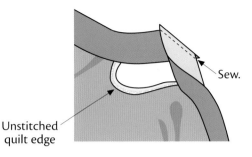

Sew.

Unstitched quilt edge

11. Place the binding back on the quilt with the raw edges aligned. Beginning and ending with a back-stitch, finish stitching the binding to the quilt.

12. Turn the binding to the back of the quilt so the raw edge of the binding meets the raw edge of the quilt. Fold the binding over again so the newly folded edge just covers the binding seam on the back.

13. Secure the binding with pins or binding clips and use thread that matches the binding to hand stitch the binding to the back of the quilt, mitering the corners.

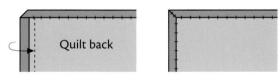

Quilt back

LABELS

This may be the last step, but I feel it is one of the most important. A quilt may be lovely to look at and fun to cuddle up in, but its value increases tremendously when its story is told. Include all the pertinent details; they will make the quilt dearer to the owner, especially with the passage of time. At the very least, a label should include the name of the quilt or pattern, the maker's name, the place where the quilt was made, and the date. Since many of these quilts are made "for someone special, by someone special," photos transferred onto the label can add the perfect touch.

Simple Muslin Labels

Handmade labels can be made quite easily by ironing a 4" x 6" rectangle of freezer paper shiny side down to the center of a 5" x 7" piece of good-quality muslin.

Write the desired information on the fabric side of the label using a fine-point permanent marker. I find it helpful to draw horizontal, parallel lines on the dull (paper) side of the freezer paper with a thicker marker. These lines shadow through to the front of the fabric and help keep my writing level.

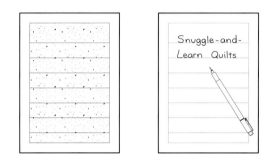

Snuggle-and-Learn Quilts

Once the label is complete, remove the freezer paper, press under ¼" on all four sides of the muslin and hand stitch the finished label to the back of the quilt.

Photo Labels

We live in a wonderful age where pictures can be printed directly onto fabric. Choose a colorfast printer fabric made from premium cotton muslin that has been backed to feed through an inkjet printer. Scan the picture into the computer, add the desired text in an attractive font, choose an appropriate border, and follow the manufacturer's instructions to print the entire image onto the colorfast printer fabric. Even if a photograph is not included, this is a great way to make an appliquéd label for your quilt!

Hanna's Critter Quilt Made with love by Grandma Chris ♥ Chris Lynn Kirsch Watertown, WI 2007

Labels in the Quilting

Here's one last exciting idea: great artists always sign the front of their work. Your quilts are your art. Add your name in free-motion quilting to the lower-right corner of your quilt in a high-contrast thread color.

On occasion, I have added the date, the name of the recipient, and anything else that tickles my fancy as part of my free-motion quilting design. What a great way to make your work of art truly one of a kind!

GALLERY OF QUILTS

Making any Snuggle-and-Learn quilt will be a great experience, but sometimes it's fun to take an idea and do something new with it. This chapter includes examples of other quilts I've made with a Snuggle-and-Learn theme, as well as quilts created by friends and students who were inspired to take my ideas to another level.

Hanna's Bedtime Quilt by Chris Lynn Kirsch. Hanna is a small doll that can be placed in the different pockets of each block as the poem is read. In this picture she is tucked in her bed in the center block. The other pockets are in the waves, bananas, tulip, and kennel, as well as in the motif in each corner of the quilt.

The Critter Quilt by Chris Lynn Kirsch.

Dutch Polish Color Quilt by Chris Lynn Kirsch and Wendy Rieves. This quilt
was made for Nina Scholten. Her daddy is Dutch and her mommy is Polish.

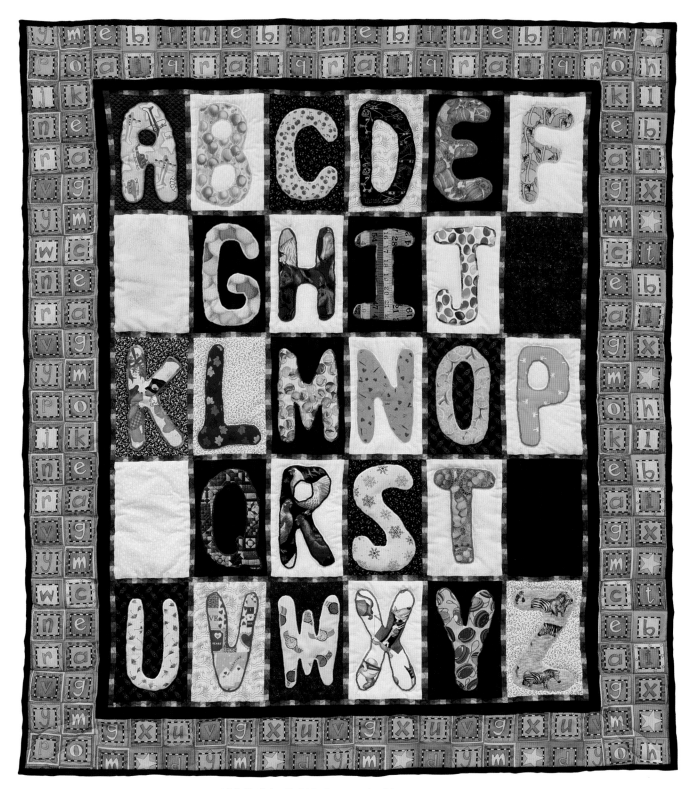

ABC Quilt by Debbie Braatz. The fabric in each letter
contains motifs that begin with that letter.

"J" is for Jacob by Mary Hedgcock. This quilt was made for Mary's grandson, Jacob. His picture is included in the center of the quilt.

Colors by Rita Harris. Rita made this quilt to keep in her home for when the grandkids come to visit.

ABOUT THE **AUTHOR**

Chris Lynn Kirsch learned to sew as a child and was taking tailoring classes by her senior year of high school. She didn't discover quiltmaking, however, until she was married and had children, and her sister-in-law, Mary Sue, talked her into taking a class. Chris began making every pattern she could find, and she created her own techniques and designs when she couldn't find the patterns she wanted. She has no background in art, so finding that she could design was a wonderful discovery.

Chris's children are now grown and beginning families of their own. Chris, her husband, Mike, and their dog, Jasmine, live in a log home in the Wisconsin woods, where Chris is blessed with a new studio and the opportunity to pursue quiltmaking full time. She currently teaches quilting at two technical colleges, at quilt shows, and for guilds and shops. She and her friend Wendy Rieves lead quilting cruises all over the world. Her quilts have won ribbons and been displayed internationally. She may be reached at www.chrisquilts.net.

Martingale®
& C O M P A N Y

America's Best-Loved Craft & Hobby Books®
America's Best-Loved Knitting Books®

That Patchwork Place®

America's Best-Loved Quilt Books®

APPLIQUÉ
Adoration Quilts
Beautiful Blooms—*New!*
Cutting-Garden Quilts
Favorite Quilts from Anka's Treasures
Mimi Dietrich's Favorite Applique Quilts
Sunbonnet Sue and Scottie Too

FOCUS ON WOOL
The Americana Collection
Needle-Felting Magic
Needle Felting with Cotton and Wool—*New!*
Simply Primitive

GENERAL QUILTMAKING
Bits and Pieces
Bound for Glory
Calendar Kids
Charmed
Christmas with Artful Offerings
Colorful Quilts
Comfort and Joy
Cool Girls Quilt
Creating Your Perfect Quilting Space
A Dozen Roses
Fig Tree Quilts: Houses
**Follow-the-Line Quilting Designs
    Volume Three—*New!***
The Little Box of Quilter's Chocolate Desserts
Points of View
Positively Postcards
Prairie Children and Their Quilts
Quilt Revival
Quilter's Block-a-Day Calendar
Quilter's Happy Hour—New!
Quilting in the Country
Sensational Sashiko
Simple Seasons
Simple Seasons Recipe Cards
Simple Traditions
Skinny Quilts and Table Runners—*New!*
Twice Quilted
Young at Heart Quilts

LEARNING TO QUILT
Color for the Terrified Quilter
Happy Endings, Revised Edition
Let's Quilt!
Your First Quilt Book (or it should be!)

PAPER PIECING
300 Paper-Pieced Quilt Blocks
Easy Machine Paper Piecing
Paper-Pieced Mini Quilts
Show Me How to Paper Piece
Showstopping Quilts to Foundation Piece
Spellbinding Quilts

PIECING
40 Fabulous Quick-Cut Quilts
Better by the Dozen
Big 'n Easy
Clever Quarters, Too
Copy Cat Quilts—*New!*
Maple Leaf Quilts—*New!*
Mosaic Picture Quilts
New Cuts for New Quilts
Nine by Nine
Quilts on the Double—*New!*
Ribbon Star Quilts—*New!*
Sew Fun, Sew Colorful Quilts
Sew One and You're Done
Snowball Quilts
Square Deal
Sudoku Quilts
Wheel of Mystery Quilts

QUILTS FOR BABIES & CHILDREN
Baby Wraps—*New!*
Even More Quilts for Baby
Lickety-Split Quilts for Little Ones
The Little Box of Baby Quilts
Quilts for Baby
Sweet and Simple Baby Quilts

SCRAP QUILTS
Nickel Quilts
Save the Scraps
Simple Strategies for Scrap Quilts

CRAFTS
101 Sparkling Necklaces
Art from the Heart
The Beader's Handbook
Card Design
Creative Embellishments
Crochet for Beaders
It's a Wrap
It's in the Details
The Little Box of Beaded Bracelets
    and Earrings
The Little Box of Beaded Necklaces
    and Earrings
Miniature Punchneedle Embroidery
A Passion for Punchneedle
Punchneedle Fun
Scrapbooking off the Page…and on
    the Wall
Sculpted Threads
Sew Sentimental
Stitched Collage—*New!*

KNITTING & CROCHET
365 Crochet Stitches a Year:
    Perpetual Calendar
365 Knitting Stitches a Year:
    Perpetual Calendar
A to Z of Knitting
Amigurumi World—*New!*
Crocheted Pursenalities
First Crochet
First Knits
Fun and Funky Crochet
Handknit Skirts
Kitty Knits—*New!*
The Knitter's Book of Finishing
    Techniques
Knitting Circles around Socks
Knitting with Gigi
The Little Box of Crocheted Throws
The Little Box of Knitted Throws
Modern Classics
More Sensational Knitted Socks
Pursenalities
Wrapped in Comfort

Our books are available at bookstores and your favorite craft,
fabric, and yarn retailers. If you don't see the title you're looking for,
visit us at **www.martingale-pub.com** or contact us at:

1-800-426-3126

International: 1-425-483-3313 • **Fax:** 1-425-486-7596 • **Email:** info@martingale-pub.com